# The Letters of L

# Lady Hamilton,

With A Supplement Of Interesting Letters By

Distinguished Characters

# (Volume II)

Viscount Horatio Nelson Nelson

# Alpha Editions

This edition published in 2022

ISBN : 9789356783454

Design and Setting By
**Alpha Editions**
www.alphaedis.com
Email - info@alphaedis.com

# The Letters of Lord Nelson to Lady Hamilton, Vol II
## by
## Viscount Horatio Nelson Nelson

# LETTER XL.

Victory, under Majorca,
January 13th, 1804.

**MY OWN DEAR BELOVED EMMA,**

I received, on the 9th, your letters of September 29th, October 2, 7, 10, 12, 17th, November 5th, 8th, to the 24th: and I am truly sensible of all your kindness and affectionate regard for me; which, I am sure, is reciprocal, in every respect, from your own Nelson.

If that Lady Bitch knew of that person's coming to her house, it was a trick; but which, I hope, you will not subject yourself to again. But, I do not like it!

However, it is passed; and, we must have confidence in each other: and, my dearest Emma, judging of you by myself, it is not all the world that could seduce me, in thought, word, or deed, from all my soul holds most dear.

Indeed, if I can help it, I never intend to go out of the ship, but to the shore of Portsmouth; and that will be, if it pleases God, before next Christmas. Indeed, I think, long before, if the French will venture to sea.

I send you a letter from the Queen of Naples. They call out, might and main, for our protection; and, God knows, they are sure of me.

Mr. Elliot complains heavily of the expence; and says, he will retire the moment it is peace. He expected his family, when they would sit down eleven Elliots!

If, my dear Emma, you are to mind all the reports you may hear, you may always be angry with your Nelson.

In the first place, instead of eight days, Mr. Acourt; he came on board one day, just before dinner, and left me next morning, after breakfast.

What pleasure people can have in telling lies! But, I care not what they say; I defy them all.

You may safely rely, that I can for ever repeat, with truth, these words—for ever I love you, and only you, my Emma; and, you may be assured, as long as you are the same to me, that you are never absent a moment from my thoughts.

I am glad you are going to Merton; you will live much more comfortable, and much cheaper, than in London: and this spring, if you like to have the house altered, you can do it. But, I fancy, you will soon tire of so much dirt, and the inconvenience will be very great the whole summer.

All I request, if you fix to have it done, [is] that Mr. Davison's architect, who drew the plan, may have the inspection; and, he must take care that it does not exceed the estimate.

If it is done by contract, you must not *alter*, or a bill is run-up, much worse than if we had never contracted. Therefore, I must either buy the materials, and employ respectable workmen, under the architect; or, contract.

I rather believe, it would be better for me to buy the materials, and put out the building to a workman; but, you must get some good advice.

With respect to the new entrance— * * * * * * * * * * * * * * * * * * * * * * * * *

## LETTER XLI.

Victory, March 14th, [1804] off Toulon.

Young Faddy, my Dearest Emma, brought me, two days ago, your dear and most kind letter of November 26th, and you are sure that I shall take a very early opportunity of promoting him; and he appears to be grown a fine young man, but vacancies do not happen very frequently in this station. However, if he behaves well, he may be sure of me.

With respect to Mr. Jefferson, I can [neither] say nor do any thing. The surgeon of the Victory is a very able, excellent man, and the ship is kept in the most perfect state of health; and, I would not, if I could—but, thank [God] I cannot—do such an unjust act, as to remove him. He is my own asking for! and, I have every reason to be perfectly content.

Mr. Jefferson got on, by my help; and, by his own misconduct, he got out of a good employ, and has seen another person, at Malta hospital, put over his head. He must now begin again; and act with much more attention and sobriety, than he has done, to ever get forward again: but, time may do much; and, I shall rejoice to hear of his reformation.

I am not surprised, my dearest Emma, at the enormous expences of the watering place; but, if it has done my own Emma service, it is well laid out. A thousand pounds a year will not go far; and we need be great economists, to make both ends meet, and to carry on the little improvements. As for making one farthing more prize-money, I do not expect it; except, by taking the French fleet: and, the event of that day, who can foresee!

With respect to Mrs. Græfer—what she has done, God and herself knows; but I have made up my mind, that Gibbs will propose an hundred pounds a year for her: if so, I shall grant it, and have done. I send you Mrs. Græfer's last letter.

Whilst I am upon the subject of Bronte, I have one word more—and your good, dear, kind heart, must not think that I shall die one hour the sooner; on the contrary, my mind has been more content ever since I have done: I have left you a part of the rental of Bronte, to be first paid every half year, and in advance. It is but common justice; and, whether Mr. Addington gives you any thing, or not, you will want it.

I would not have you lay out more than is necessary, at Merton. The rooms, and the new entrance, will take a good deal of money. The entrance by the corner I would have certainly done; a common white gate will do for the present; and one of the cottages, which is in the barn, can be put up, as a temporary lodge. The road can be made to a temporary bridge; for that part of the *Nile*, one day, shall be filled up.

Downing's canvas awning will do for a passage. For the winter, the carriage can be put in the barn; and, giving up Mr. Bennett's premises, will save fifty pounds a year: and, another year, we can fit up the coach-house and stables, which are in the barn.

The foot-path should be turned. I did shew Mr. Haslewood the way I wished it done; and Mr. ——— will have no objections, if we make it better than ever it has been: and, I also beg, as my dear Horatia is to be at Merton, that a strong netting, about three feet high, may be placed round the Nile, that the little thing may not tumble in; and, then, you may have ducks again in it. I forget, at what place we saw the netting; and either Mr. Perry, or Mr. Goldsmid, told us where it was to be bought. I shall be very anxious until I know this is done.

I have had no very late opportunities of sending to Naples: but, *via* Malta, I wrote to Gibbs, to desire he would send over and purchase the *amorins*. They will arrive in time. I hope, the watch is arrived safe.

The British Fair cutter, I hope, is arrived safe. She has three packets, from me, to England,

The expences of the alterations at Merton *you are* not to pay from the income. Let it all be put to a separate account, and I will provide a fund for the payment.

All I long for, just now, is to hear that you are *perfectly* recovered; and, then, I care for nothing: all my hopes are, to see you, and be happy, at dear Merton, again; but, I fear, this miscarriage of Pichegru's, in France, will prolong the war. It has kept the French fleet in port, which we are all sorry for.

Sir William Bolton was on board yesterday. He looks thin. The fag in a brig is very great; and I see no prospect of his either making prize-money, or being made post, at present: but, I shall omit no opportunity.

I wrote to Mrs. Bolton a few months ago; and gave her letter, yesterday, to Bolton. He conducts himself very well, indeed.

Ever, my dearest Emma, for ever, I am your most faithful, and affectionate

NELSON & BRONTE.

Although I cannot well afford it, yet I could not bear that poor blind Mrs. Nelson should be in want in her old days, and sell her plate; therefore, if you will find out what are her debts, if they come within my power, I will certainly pay them.

Many, I dare say, if they had commanded here, would have made money; but, I can assure you, for prizes taken within the Mediterranean, I have not more than paid my expences. However, I would rather pinch myself, than she, poor soul, should want. Your good, angelic heart, my dearest beloved Emma, will fully agree with me, every thing is very expensive; and, even we find it, and will be obliged to economise, if we assist our friends: and, I am sure, we should feel more comfort in it than in loaded tables, and entertaining a set of people who care not for us.

An account is this moment brought me, that a small sum is payable to me, for some neutral taken off Cadiz in May 1800; so that I shall not be poorer for my gift. It is odd, is it not?

I shall, when I come home, settle four thousand pounds in trustees hands, for Horatia; for, I will not put it in my own power to have her left destitute: for she would want friends, if we left her in this world. She shall be independent of any smiles or frowns!

I am glad you are going to take her home; and, if you will take the trouble with Eliza and Ann, I am the very last to object.

Tom, I shall certainly assist at college; and, I am sure, the Doctor expects that I should do the same for Horace: but I must make my arrangements, so as not to run in debt.

April 9th.

I have wrote to the Duke; but, by your account, I fear he is not alive. I write, because you wish me; and, because I like the Duke, and hope he will leave you some money. But, for myself, I can have no right to expect a farthing: nor would I be a legacy hunter for the world; I never knew any good come from it.

I send you a letter from Mr. Falconet. I am afraid, they have made a jumble about the *amorins*. And I send you a very impertinent letter from that old cat. I have sent her a very dry answer, and told her, I should send the sweetmeats to you. I always hated the old bitch! But, was she young, and as beautiful as an angel, I am engaged; I am all, soul and body, my Emmas: nor would I change her for all this world could give me.

I would not have Horatia think of a dog. I shall not bring her one; and, I am sure, she is better without a pet of that sort. But, she is like her mother, would get all the old dogs in the place about her.

April 14th.

I am so sea-sick, that I cannot write another line; except, to say—God Almighty bless you, my dearest beloved Emma! prays, ever, your faithful

NELSON & BRONTE.

## LETTER XLII.

Victory, April 2d, 1804.

I have, my Dearest Beloved Emma, been so uneasy for this last month; desiring, most ardently, to hear of your well doing!

Captain Capel brought me your letters, sent by the Thisbe, from Gibraltar. I opened—opened—found none but December, and early in January. I was in such an agitation! At last, I found one without a date: which, thank God! told my poor heart, that you was recovering; but, that dear little Emma was no more! and, that Horatia had been so very ill—it all together upset me.

But, it was just at bed-time; and I had time to reflect, and be thankful to God for sparing you and our dear Horatia. I am sure, the loss of one— much more, both—would have drove me mad. I was so agitated, as it was, that I was glad it was night, and that I could be by myself.

Kiss dear Horatia, for me: and tell her, to be a dutiful and good child; and, if she is, that we shall always love her.

You may, if you like, tell Mrs. G. that I shall certainly settle a small pension on her. It shall not be large, as we may have the pleasure of making her little presents; and, my dearest Emma, I shall not be wanting to every body who has been kind to you, be they servants or gentlefolks.

Admiral Lutwidge is a good man; and, I like Mrs. Lutwidge—and shall, always more, because she is fond of you.

Never mind the great Bashaw at the Priory. He be damned! If he was single, and had a mind to marry you, he could only make you a

Marchioness: but, as he is situated, and I situated, I can make you a Duchess; and, if it pleases God, that time may arrive! Amen. Amen.

As for your friend Lady H———, she is, in her way, as great a pimp as any of them.

What a set! But, if they manage their own intrigues, is not that enough! I am sure, neither you or I care what they do; much less, envy them their *chere amies*.

As for Lord S———, and the other, I care nothing about them; for I have every reason, by my own feelings towards you, to think you care only for your Nelson.

I have not heard of your receiving the little box from Naples; bracelets, I fancy, but I did not open them.

I wish the *amorins* may come in time for the conveyance of Captain Layman; who has, most unfortunately, lost his sloop: he is strongly recommended, by the governor and garrison of Gibraltar. But, perhaps, he may not be able to obtain it.

We have such reports about the King's health, that the present ministry may be out; and, for what I know or care, another set may be no better, for you or me.

As for the Admiralty, let who will be in, they can neither do me any great good or harm: they may vex me, a little; but, that will recoil upon themselves.

I hope, however, they will confirm Captain Layman; for he is attached not only to me, but is a very active officer. But, it was his venturing to know more about India than Troubridge, that made them look shy upon him; and, his tongue runs too fast. I often tell him, not to let his tongue run so fast, or his pen write so much.

## LETTER XLIII.

Victory, off Toulon,
April 10th, 1804.

**MY DEAREST EMMA,**

I have received all your truly kind and affectionate letters, to January 25th, by the Thisbe; and, last night, your letter of January 13th, by Naples.

The *amorins* will go under the care of Captain Layman; who, unfortunately, lost his sloop: but, with much credit to himself, he has been acquitted of all blame.

I rejoice that dear Horatia is got well; and, also, that you, my dearest Emma, are recovered of your severe indisposition.

In our present situation with Spain, this letter, probably, may never reach you. I have wrote fully; and intend to send them by the Argus, who I expect to join every minute.

Elphi Bey, I hear, has had all his fine things taken from him. He escaped into the Desert, and is pursued; probably, his head is off, long before this time.

The French fleet came out on the 5th, but went in again the next morning.

Yesterday, a Rear-Admiral, and seven sail of ships, including frigates, put their nose outside the harbour. If they go on playing this game, some day we shall lay salt upon their tails; and so end the campaign of, my dearest Emma, your most faithful and affectionate

––––––––––

I am glad to hear that you are going to take my dear Horatia, to educate her. She must turn out an angel, if she minds what you say to her; and Eliza and Ann will never forget your goodness.

My health is *so, so*! I shall get through the summer; and, in the winter, shall go home.

You will readily fancy all I would say, and do think.

My kind love to all friends.

## LETTER XLIV.

Victory, April 19th, 1804.

**MY DEAREST EMMA,**

I had wrote you a line, intended for the Swift cutter; but, instead of her joining me, I had the mortification, not only to hear that she was taken, but that *all* the dispatches and letters had fallen into the hands of the enemy; a very pretty piece of work!

I am not surprised at the capture; but am very much so, that any dispatches should be sent in a vessel with twenty-three men, not equal to cope with any row-boat privateer.

As I do not know what letters of your's are in her, I cannot guess what will be said. I suppose, there will be a publication.

The loss of the Hindostan, was great enough; but, for importance, it is lost, in comparison to the probable knowledge the enemy will obtain of our connections with foreign countries! Foreigners for ever say—and it is true—"We dare not trust England; one way, or other, we are sure to be committed!" However, it is now too late to launch out on this subject.

Not a thing has been saved out of the Hindostan, not a second shirt for any one; and it has been by extraordinary exertions, that the people's lives were saved.

Captain Hallowell is so good as to take home, for me, wine as by the inclosed list; and, if I can, some honey. The Spanish honey is so precious, that if [any one has] a cut, or sore throat, it is used to cure it. I mention this, in case you should wish to give the Duke a jar. The smell is wonderful! It is to be produced no where, but in the mountains near Rosas.

The Cyprus wine, one hogshead, was for Buonaparte.

I would recommend the wine-cooper drawing it off: and you can send a few dozens to the Duke; who, I know, takes a glass every day at two o'clock.

I wish, I had any thing else to send you; but, my dearest Emma, you must take the will for the deed.

I am pleased with Charlotte's letter; and, as she loves my dear Horatia, I shall always like her.

What hearts those must have, who do not! But, thank God, she shall not be dependent on any of them.

Your letter of February 12th, through Mr. Falconet, I have received. I know, they are all read; therefore, never sign your name. I shall continue to write, through Spain; but never say a word that can convey any information—except, of eternal attachment and affection for you; and that, I care not, who knows; for I am, for ever, and ever, your, only your,

NELSON & BRONTE.

Poor Captain Le Gros had your note to him in his pocket-book, and that was all he saved.

Mr. Este left him at Gibraltar, and went to Malta in the Thisbe.

Captain Le Gros is now trying. I think, it will turn out, that every person is obliged to his conduct for saving their lives.

She took fire thirteen leagues from the land.

# LETTER XLV.

Victory, April 23,1804.

**MY DEAREST EMMA,**

Hallowell has promised me, if the *Admiralty* will give him leave to go to London, that he will call at Merton.

His spirit is certainly more independent than almost any man's I ever knew; but, I believe, he is attached to me. I am sure, he has no reason to be so, to either Troubridge or any one at the Admiralty.

I have sent, last night, a box of Marischino Veritabile of Zara, which I got Jemmy Anderson to buy for me, and twelve bottles of *tokay*. I have kept none for myself, being better pleased that you should have it.

I am, ever, and for ever, your most faithful and affectionate

NELSON & BRONTE.

Hallowell parted last night; but, being in sight, I am sending a frigate with a letter to the Admiralty.

May God Almighty bless you, and send us a happy meeting!

# LETTER XLVI.

Victory, May 5, 1804.

I find, my Dearest Emma, that your picture is very much admired by the French Consul at Barcelona; and that he has not sent it to be admired— which, I am sure, it would be—by Buonaparte.

They pretend, that there were three pictures taken. I wish, I had them: but they are all gone, as irretrievably as the dispatches; unless we may read them in a book, as we printed their correspondence from Egypt.

But, from us, what can they find out! That I love you, most dearly; and hate the French, most damnably.

Dr. Scott went to Barcelona, to try to get the private letters; but, I fancy, they are all gone to Paris. The Swedish and American Consuls told him, that the French Consul had your picture, and read your letters; and, Doctor thinks, one of them probably read the letters.

By the master's account of the cutter, I would not have trusted a pair of old shoes in her. He tells me, she did not sail, but was a good sea-boat.

I hope, Mr. Marsden will not trust any more of my private letters in such a conveyance; if they choose to trust the affairs of the public in such a thing, I cannot help it.

I long for the invasion being over; it must finish the war, and I have no fears for the event.

I do not say, all I wish; and which, my dearest *beloved* Emma—(read that, whoever opens this letter; and, for what I care, publish it to the world)—your fertile imagination can readily fancy I would say: but this I can say, with great truth, that I am, FOR EVER, YOUR'S

---

## LETTER XLVII.

Victory, May 27th, 1804.

### MY DEAREST EMMA,

Yesterday, I took Charles Connor on board, from the Phoebe, to try what we can do with him. At present, poor fellow, he has got a very bad eye—and, I almost fear, that he will be blind of it—owing to an olive-stone striking his eye: but the surgeon of the Victory, who is by far the most able medical man I have ever seen, and equally so as a surgeon, [says] that, if it can be saved, he will do it.

The other complaint, in his head, is but little more, I think, than it was when he first came to Deal; a kind of silly laugh, when spoken to. He always complains of a pain in the back part of his head; but, when that is gone, I do not perceive but that he is as wise as many of his neighbours.

You may rely, my dear Emma, that nothing shall be wanting, on my part, to render him every service.

Capel—although, I am sure, very kind to younkers—I do not think, has the knack of keeping them in high discipline; he lets them be their own master too much.

I paid Charles's account, yesterday; since he has been in the Phoebe, one hundred and fifty-five pounds, fourteen shillings. However, he must now turn over a new leaf; and I sincerely hope, poor fellow, he will yet do well.

I wrote you on the 22d, through Rosas, in Spain; and I shall write, in a few days, by Barcelona: this goes by Gibraltar.

I have wrote Admiral Lutwidge; Mrs. Lutwidge must wait, for I cannot get through all my numerous letters: for, whoever writes, although upon their own affairs, are offended if they are not answered.

I have not seen young Bailey: I suppose, he is in the Leviathan. By the parcel, I see, he is in the Canopus; and I can, at present, be of no use to him.

May 30th.

Charles is very much recovered.

I write you, this day, by Barcelona. Your dear phiz—but not the least like you—on the cup, is safe: but I would not use it, for the world; for, if it was broke, it would distress me very much.

Your letters, by Swift, I shall never get back. The French Consul, at Barcelona, is bragging that he has three pictures of you from the Swift.

I do not believe him; but, what if he had a hundred! Your resemblance is so deeply engraved in my heart, that there it can never be effaced: and, who knows? some day, I may have the happiness of having a living picture of you!

Old Mother L—— is a damned b——: but I do not understand what you mean, or what plan.

I am not surprised at my friend Kingsmill admiring you, and forgetting Mary; he loves variety, and handsome women.

You touch upon the old Duke; but, I am dull of comprehension: believing you all my own, I cannot imagine any one else to offer, in any way.

We have enough, with prudence; and, without it, we should soon be beggars, if we had five times as much.

I see, Lord Stafford is going to oppose Mr. Addington; the present ministry cannot stand.

I wish Mr. Addington had given you the pension; Pitt, and hard-hearted Grenville, never will.

What a fortune the death of Lord Camelford gives him!

Every thing you tell me about my dear Horatia charms me. I think I see her, hear her, and admire her; but, she is like her dear, dear mother.

I am sorry, if your account of George Martin's wife is correct; he deserved a better fate. But, he is like Foley; gave up a great deal, to marry the relation of a great man: although, in fact, she is no relation to the Duke of Portland.

I wish, I could but be at dear Merton, to assist in making the alterations. I think, I should have persuaded you to have kept the pike, and a clear stream; and to have put all the carp, tench, and fish who muddy the water, into the pond. But, as you like, I am content. Only take care, that my darling does not fall in, and get drowned. I begged you to get the little netting along the edge; and, particularly, on the bridges.

I admire the seal; and God bless you, also! Amen.

The boy, South, is on board another ship, learning to be a musician. He will return soon, when he shall have the letter and money. I hope, he will deserve it; but he has been a very bad boy: but good floggings, I hope, will save him from the gallows.

Mr. Falcon is a clever man. He would not have made such a blunder as our friend Drake, and Spencer Smith. I hear, the last is coming, *viâ* Trieste, to Malta. Perhaps, he wants to get to Constantinople; and, if the Spencers get in, the Smiths will get any thing.

Mr. Elliot, I hear, is a candidate for it. He complains of the expence of Naples, I hear; and, that he cannot make both ends meet, although he sees no company.

The histories of the Queen are beyond whatever I have heard from Sir William. Prince Leopold's establishment is all French. The Queen's favourite, Lieutenant-Colonel St. Clair, was a subaltern; La Tour, the Captain in the navy; and, another!

However, I never touch on these matters; for, I care not how she amuses herself.

It will be the upset of Acton; or, rather, he will not, I am told, stay.

The King is angry with her; his love is long gone by.

I have only one word more—Do not believe a syllable the newspapers say, or what you hear. Mankind seems fond of telling lies.

Remember me kindly to Mrs. Cadogan, and all our mutual friends; and be assured, I am, for ever, my dearest Emma, your most faithful and affectionate

NELSON & BRONTE.

George Campbell desires me always to present his best respects; and make mine to good Mr. Yonge. What can I write him? I am sure, he must have great pleasure in attending you: and, when you see Sir William Scott, make my best regards acceptable to him. There is no man I have a higher opinion of, both as a public and private character.

You will long ago have had my letter; with one to Davison, desiring he will pay for the alterations at Merton. I shall send you a letter for the hundred pounds a month, to the Bank.

# LETTER XLVIII.

Victory, June 6th, 1804.

Since I wrote you, my Dearest Emma, on the 30th and 31st May, nothing new has happened; except our hearing the *feu de joie* at Toulon, for the declaration of Emperor.

What a capricious nation those French must be! However, I think it must, in any way, be advantageous to England. There ends, for a century, all republics!

By vessels from Marseilles, the French think it will be a peace; and they say, that several of their merchant ships are fitting out. I earnestly pray, that it may be so; and, that we may have a few years of rest.

I rather believe, my antagonist at Toulon, begins to be angry with me: at least, I am trying to make him so; and then, he may come out, and beat me, as he says he did, off Boulogne.

He is the Admiral that went to Naples in December 1792, La Touche Treville, who landed the grenadiers. I owe him something for that.

I am better, my dear Emma, than I have been, and shall get through the summer very well; and I have the pleasure to tell you, that Charles is very much recovered. There is no more the matter with his intellects, than with mine! Quite the contrary; he is very quick.

Mr. Scott, who has overlooked all his things, says, his clothes, &c. are in the highest order he has ever seen.

I shall place him in the Niger, with Captain Hilliar, when he joins; but, all our ships are so full, that it is very difficult to get a birth for one in any ship.

Would you conceive it possible! but, it is now from April 2d, since I have heard direct from Ball. The average time for a frigate to go, and return, is from six to seven weeks.

From you, I had letters, April 5th, and the papers to April 8th, received May 10th, with a convoy.

This goes through friend Gayner.

Sir William Bolton joined last night; and received his letters, announcing his being called *papa*. He is got a very fine young man and good officer.

Lord St. Vincent has desired he may have the first Admiralty vacancy for post; but nobody will die, or go home.

*A-propos!* I believe, you should buy a piece of plate, value fifty pounds, for our god-daughter of Lady Bolton; and something of twenty or thirty pounds value, for Colonel Suckling's.

But, my Emma, you are not to pay for them, let it rest for me; or, if the amount is sent me, I will order payment.

Remember me most kindly to Horatia, good Mrs. Cadogan, Charlotte, Miss Connor, and all our friends at dear, dear Merton; where, from my soul, I wish I was, this moment: then, I sincerely hope, we should have no cause for sorrow.

You will say what is right to Mr. Perry, Newton, Patterson, Mr. Lancaster, &c. you know all these matters. God in Heaven bless and preserve you, for ever! prays, ever, your's most faithfully,

---

## LETTER XLIX.

Victory, June 10th, 1804.

### MY DEAREST EMMA,

I wrote to you, on the 6th, *viâ* Rosas: this goes by Barcelona; to which place I am sending Sir William Bolton, to fetch Dr. Scott, who is gone there, poor fellow, for the benefit of his health!

I have just had very melancholy letters from the King and Queen of Naples, on account of General Acton's going to Sicily.

The insolence of Buonaparte was not to be parried without a war; for which they are unable, if unassisted.

I have letters from Acton, May 28, on board the Archimedes, just going into Palermo. He will probably return to Naples, unless new events arise: and that may be; for a minister, once out, may find some difficulty in renewing his post. He has acted with great and becoming spirit.

I am better, but I have been very unwell. It blows, here, as much as ever. Yesterday was a little hurricane of wind.

I dare say, Prince Castelcicala knows it by express; if not, you may tell him, with my best respects. He, and every one else, may be sure of my attachment to those good sovereigns. By this route, I do not choose to say more on this subject.

With my kindest regards to Horatia and your good mother, Charlotte, Miss C. and all our friends, believe me, my dear Emma, for ever, your most faithful and affectionate

————

I fear, Sardinia will be invaded from Corsica before you get this letter. I have not small ships to send there, or any where else; not in the proportion of one to five.

You may communicate this to Mr. Addington, if you think that he does not know it; but, to no one else, except Castelcicala, of what relates to Naples.

I have very flattering letters from the Grand Vizier, in the name of the Sultan; and from Cadir, now Capitan Pacha.

## LETTER L.

Victory, July 1st, 1804.

Although I have wrote you, my dearest Emma, a letter, by Rosas, of June 27th, not yet gone, the weather being so very bad, that ships cannot get across the Gulph of Lyons, yet I will [not] miss the opportunity of writing by Gibraltar.

You must not, my Emma, think of hearing from me by way of Malta; it takes as long to send a letter to Malta, as to England.

The Monmouth, which you complain of not hearing by, I knew nothing of her movements for some months before. The ships from Malta, with the convoys, pick up our letters at Gibraltar. Therefore, do not hurt my feelings, by telling me that I neglect any opportunity of writing.

Your letters of April 13th, 22d, and May 13th, through Mr. Falconet, came safe, a few days ago. Mr. Falconet is the French banker; and he dare not buy a little macaroni for me, or let an Englishman into his house.

Gibbs is still at Palermo: I fancy, he will make a good thing of my estate; however, I wish it was settled. He wrote me, a short time since, that he wished I would give him a hint (but without noticing that it came from him) that I thought Mrs. Græfer and her child had better go to England; on pretence of educating her daughter, &c.

But I would have nothing to do with any such recommendation. It would end in her coming to me, in England; and saying, that she could not live upon what she had, and that I advised her to come to England, or she should not have thought of it.

In short, Gibbs wants to remove her. He is afraid of his pocket, I fancy; and the daughter is, I fancy, now in some seminary at Palermo, at Gibbs's expence.

I wrote him word, fully, I would advise no such thing; she was to form her own judgment.

What our friends are after at Naples, they best know. The poor King is miserable at the loss of Acton.

The Queen writes me about honest Acton, &c. &c. and I hear, that she has been the cause of ousting him: and they say—her enemies—that her conduct is all French. That, I do not believe; although she is likely to be the dupe of French emigrés, who always beset her.

I doubt much, my dear Emma, even her constancy of real friendship to you; although, in my letter to Acton, which Mr. Elliot says he read to her, I mentioned the obligations she was under to you, &c. &c. in very strong terms.

What could the name of the minister signify! It was the letter which was wanted to the Prime-Minister.

But, never mind; with prudence, we shall do very well.

I have wrote to Davison, by land: who, I am very sorry for; but, he never would take a friend's caution, and he has been severely bit.

Your accounts of Merton delight me; and you will long ago have known, that I have directed the bills for the alterations to be paid. I never could have intended to have taken it from the hundred pounds a month.

You will not hear of my making prize-money. I have not paid my expences these last nine months.

I shall expect to eat my Christmas dinner at Merton; unless those events happen which I can neither foresee nor prevent.

I am not well: and must have rest, for a few months, even should the country [want me;] which, very likely, they will not. News, I can have none. April 9th, Leviathan sailed; so government don't care much for us.

Kiss my dear Horatia, for me! I hope you will have her at Merton; and, believe me, my dear Emma, that I am, for ever, as ever, your attached, faithful, and affectionate,

NELSON & BRONTE.

# LETTER LI.

Victory, August 12th, 1804.

Although, my Dearest Emma, from the length of time my other letters have been getting to you, I cannot expect that this will share a better fate; yet, as the Childers is going to Rosas, to get us some news from Paris—which is the only way I know of what is passing in England—I take my chance of the post: but, I expect the Kent will be in England before this letter; and by which ship I write to the Admiralty relative to my health.

Therefore, I shall only say, that I hope a little of your good nursing, with ass's milk, will set me up for another campaign; should the Admiralty wish me to return, in the spring, for another year: but, I own, I think we shall have peace.

The Ambuscade arrived this day fortnight, with our victuallers, &c. and very acceptable they were. By her, I received your letters of May 14th, 22d, and 30th, *viâ* Lisbon; and, of April 9th, 18, 15th, May 10th, 18th, 29th, June 1st, 5th, through, I suppose, the Admiralty.

The box you mention, is not arrived; nor have I a scrap of a pen from Davison. The weather in the Mediterranean seems much altered. In July, seventeen days the fleet was in a gale of wind.

I have often wrote to Davison, to pay for all the improvements at Merton. The new-building the chamber over the dining-room, you must consider. The stair window, we settled, was not to be stopped up. The underground passage will, I hope, be made; but I shall, please God, soon see it all.

I have wrote you, my dear Emma, about Horatia; but, by the Kent, I shall write fully. May God bless you, my dearest best-beloved Emma! and believe me, ever, your most faithful and affectionate

---

Kind love, and regards, to Mrs. Cadogan, and all friends. God bless you, again and again!

# LETTER LII.

Victory, August 20th, 1804.

**MY DEAREST EMMA,**

The Kent left us three days ago; and, as the wind has been perfectly fair since her departure, I think she will have a very quick passage, and arrive long before this letter. But, as a ship is going to Rosas, I will not omit the opportunity of writing through Spain; as, you say, the letters all arrive safe.

We have nothing but gales of wind; and I have had, for two days, fires in the cabin, to keep out the very damp air.

I still hope that, by the time of my arrival in England, we shall have peace. God send it!

I have not yet received your muff; I think, probably, I shall bring it with me.

I hope, Davison has done the needful, in paying for the alterations at Merton. If not, it is now too late; and we will fix a complete plan, and execute it next summer. I shall be clear of debt, and what I have will be my own.

God bless you! Amen. Amen.

George Elliot goes to Malta, for a convoy to England, this day. If you ever see Lord Minto, say so.

---

## LETTER LIII.

Victory, August 31st, 1804—Say 30th, at Evening. Therefore, I wrote, in fact, this Day, through Spain.

**MY EVER DEAREST EMMA,**

Yesterday, I wrote to you, through Spain; this goes by Naples. Mr. Falconet, I think, will send it; although, I am sure, he feels great fear from the French minister, for having any thing to do with us.

Mr. Greville is a shabby fellow! It never could have been the intention of Sir William, but that you should have had seven hundred pounds a year neat money; for, when he made the will, the Income Tax was double to what it is at present; and the estate which it is paid from is increasing every year in value.

It may be law, but it is not just; nor in equity would, I believe, be considered as the will and intention of Sir William. Never mind! Thank God, you do not want any of his kindness; nor will he give you justice.

I may fairly say all this; because my actions are different, even to a person who has treated me so ill.

As to ——, I know the full extent of the obligation I owe him, and he may be useful to me again; but I can never forget his unkindness to you.

- 20 -

But, I guess, many reasons influenced his conduct, in bragging of his riches, and my honourable poverty; but, as I have often said, and with honest pride, what I have is my own; it never cost the widow a tear, or the nation a farthing. I got what I have with my pure blood, from the enemies of my country. Our house, my own Emma, is built upon a solid foundation; and will last to us, when his house and lands may belong to others than *his children*.

I would not have believed it, from any one but you! But, if ever I go abroad again, matters shall be settled very differently.

I am working hard with Gibbs about Bronte, but the calls upon me are very heavy. Next September, I shall be clear; I mean, September 1805.

I have wrote to both Acton and the Queen about you. I do not think she likes Mr. Elliot; and, therefore, I wish she had never shewn him my letters about you. We also know, that he has a card of his own to play.

Dr. Scott, who is a good man—although, poor fellow! very often wrong in the head—is going with Staines, in, the Cameleon, just to take a peep at Naples and Palermo. I have introduced him to Acton, who is very civil to every body from me.

The Admiralty proceedings towards me, you will know much sooner than I shall. I hope they will do the thing, handsomely, and allow of my return in the spring; but, I do not expect it.

I am very uneasy at your and Horatia being on the coast: for you cannot move, if the French make the attempt; which, I am told, they have done, and been repulsed. Pray God, it may be true!

I shall rejoice to hear you and Horatia are safe at Merton; and happy shall I be, the day I join you. *Gannam Justem.*

Gaetano is very grateful for your remembrance of him. Mr. Chevalier is an excellent servant. William says, he has wrote twice; I suppose, he thinks that enough.

This is written within three miles of the fleet in Toulon, who are looking very tempting. Kind regards to Mrs. Cadogan, Charlotte, &c. and compliments to all our joint friends; for they are no friends of mine, who are not friends to Emma.

God bless you, again and again!

Captain Hardy has not been very well: and, I fancy, Admiral Murray will not be sorry to see England; especially, since he has been promoted * * * * * * * * * * * * * * he expects his flag may get up.

God bless you, my dearest Emma; and, be assured, I am ever most faithfully your's.

---

## LETTER LIV.

Victory, September 29th, 1804.

This day, my dearest Emma, which gave me birth, I consider as more fortunate than common days; as, by my coming into this world, it has brought me so intimately acquainted with you, who my soul holds most dear. I well know that you will keep it, and have my dear Horatia to drink my health. Forty-six years of toil and trouble! How few more, the common lot of mankind leads us to expect; and, therefore, it is almost time to think of spending the few last years in peace and quietness!

By this time, I should think, either my successor is named, or permission is granted me to come home; and, if so, you will not long receive this letter before I make my appearance: which will make us, I am sure, both truly happy.

We have had nothing, for this fortnight, but gales of easterly winds, and heavy rains; not a vessel of any kind, or sort, joined the fleet.

I was in hopes Dr. Scott would have returned from Naples; and that I could have told you something comfortable for you, from that quarter: and it is now seven weeks since we heard from Malta. Therefore, I know nothing of what is passing in the world.

I would not have you, my dear Emma, allow the work of brick and mortar to go on in the winter months. It can all be finished next summer; when, I hope, we shall have peace, or such an universal war as will upset that vagabond, Buonaparte.

I have been tolerable well, till this last bad weather, which has given me pains in my breast; but, never mind, all will be well when I get to Merton.

Admiral Campbell, who is on board, desires to be remembered to you. He does not like much to stay here, after my departure. Indeed, we all draw so well together in the fleet, that I flatter myself the sorrow for my departure will be pretty general.

Admiral Murray will be glad to get home; Hardy is as good as ever; and Mr. Secretary Scott is an excellent man.

God bless you, my dearest Emma! and, be assured, I am ever your most faithful and affectionate

N. & B.

Kiss dear Horatia. I hope she is at Merton, *fixed*.

## LETTER LV.

Victory, October 7, [1804.] 2 P.M.

I wrote you, my Dearest Emma, this morning, by way of Lisbon; but a boat, which is going to Torbay, having brought out a cargo of potatoes, will I think get home before the Lisbon packet. I shall only say—*Guzelle Gannam Justem*—and that I love you beyond all the world! This may be read by French, Dutch, Spanish, or Englishmen; for it comes from the heart of, my Emma, your faithful and affectionate

NELSON & BRONTE.

I think the gentry will soon come out. I cannot say more by such a conveyance.

## LETTER LVI.

Victory, October 13, 1804.

**MY DEAREST EMMA,**

The dreadful effects of the yellow fever, at Gibraltar, and many parts of Spain, will naturally give you much uneasiness; till you hear that, thank God, we are entirely free from it, and in the most perfect health, not one man being ill in the fleet. The cold weather will, I hope, cure the disorder.

Whilst I am writing this letter, a cutter is arrived from England with strong indications of a Spanish war.

I hope, from my heart, that it will not prove one. But, however that is, my die is cast; and, long before this time, I expect, another Admiral is far on his way to supersede me. Lord Keith, I think a very likely man.

I should, for your sake, and for many of our friends, have liked an odd hundred thousand pounds; but, never mind. If they give me the choice of staying a few months longer, it will be very handsome; and, for the sake of others, we would give up, my dear Emma, very much of our own felicity. If they do not, we shall be happy with each other, and with dear Horatia.

The cutter returns with my answers directly; therefore, my own Emma, you must only fancy all my thoughts and feelings towards you. They are every thing which a fond heart can fancy.

I have not a moment; I am writing and signing orders, whilst I am writing to my own Emma.

My life, my soul, God in Heaven bless you!

Your letter is September 16th, your last is August 27th.

I have not made myself understood, about Mrs. Bolton's money. You give away *too* much.

Kiss our dear Horatia a thousand times, for your own faithful Nelson. I send two hundred pounds, keep it for your own pocket money.

You must tell Davison, and Haslewood, that I cannot answer their letters. Linton cannot be fixed; but you will know whether I come home, or stay, from Mr. Marsden.

God bless you!

Tell my brother, that I have made Mr. Yonge a Lieutenant, into the Sea-horse frigate, Captain Boyle.

Once more, God bless my dearest Emma!

———————

Write your name on the back of the bill, if you send any person for the money.

I have scrawled three lines to Davison, that he should not think I neglected him in his confinement.

I have received the inclosed from Allen. Can we assist the poor foolish man with a *character?*

## LETTER LVII.

Victory, November 23,1804.

As all our communication with Spain is at an end, I can now only expect to hear from my own dear Emma by the very slow mode of Admiralty vessels, and it is now more than two months since the John Bull sailed.

I much fear, something has been taken; for they never would, I am sure, have kept me so long in the dark. However, by management, and a portion of good luck, I got the account from Madrid in a much shorter space of time than I could have hoped for; and I have set the whole Mediterranean to work, and think the fleet cannot fail of being successful: and, if I had had the spare troops at Malta at my disposal, Minorca would at this moment have had English colours flying.

This letter, my dearest beloved Emma, goes—although in Mr. Marsden's letter—such a roundabout way, that I cannot say all that my heart wishes. Imagine every thing which is kind and affectionate, and you will come near the mark.

Where is my successor? I am not a little surprised at his not arriving! A Spanish war, I thought, would have hastened him. Ministers could not have thought that I wanted to fly the service, my whole life has proved the contrary; and, if they refuse me now: I shall most certainly leave this country in March or April; for a few months rest I must have, very soon. If I am in my grave, what are the mines of Peru to me!

But, to say the truth, I have no idea of killing myself. I may, with care, live yet to do good service to the state. My cough is very bad; and my side, where I was struck on the 14th of February, is very much swelled; at times, a lump as large as my fist, brought on, occasionally, by violent coughing: but, I hope, and believe, my lungs are yet safe.

Sir William Bolton is just arrived from Malta. I am preparing to send him a cruise, where he will have the best chance I can give him of making ten thousand pounds. He is a very attentive, good, young man.

I have not heard from Naples this age. I have, in fact, no small craft to send for news.

If I am soon to go home, I shall be with you before this letter.

May God bless you!

Thomson desires to be most kindly remembered to his dear wife and children. He is most sincerely attached to them; and wishes to save what he can for their benefit.

As our means of communicating are cut off, I have only to beg that you will not believe the idle rumours of battles, &c. &c. &c.

May Heavens bless you! prays, fervently, my dear Emma, ever your most faithful and affectionate

NELSON & BRONTE.

# LETTER LVIII.

Victory, March 9th, 1805.

I do assure you, my Dearest Emma, that nothing can be more miserable, or unhappy, than your poor Nelson.

From the 19th of February, have we been beating from Malta to off Palma; where I am now anchored, the wind and sea being so very contrary and bad. But I cannot help myself, and no one in the fleet can feel what I do: and, to mend my fate, yesterday Captain Layman arrived—to my great surprise—not in his brig, but in a Spanish cartel; he having been wrecked off Cadiz, and lost all the dispatches and letters.

You will conceive my disappointment! It is now from November 2d, that I have had a line from England.

Captain Layman says—he is sure the letters are sunk, never to rise again; but, as they were not thrown overboard until the vessel struck the rock, I have much fear that they may have fallen into the hands of the Dons.

My reports from off Toulon, state the French fleet as still in port; but, I shall ever be uneasy at not having fallen in with them.

I know, my dear Emma, that it is in vain to repine; but my feelings are alive to meeting those fellows, after near two years hard service.

What a time! I could not have thought it possible that I should have been so long absent; unwell, and uncomfortable, in many respects.

However, when I calculate upon the French fleet's not coming to sea for this summer, I shall certainly go for dear England, and a thousand [times] dearer Merton. May Heavens bless you, my own Emma!

I cannot think where Sir William Bolton is got to; he ought to have joined me, before this time.

I send you a trifle, for a birth-day's gift. I would to God, I could give you more; but, I have it not!

I get no prize-money worth naming; but, if I have the good fortune to meet the French fleet, I hope they will make me amends for all my anxiety; which has been, and is, indescribable.

How is my dear Horatia? I hope you have her under your guardian wing, at Merton. May God bless her!

Captain Layman is now upon his trial. I hope he will come clear, with honour. I fear, it was too great confidence in his own judgment that got him into the scrape; but it was impossible that any person living could have exerted himself more, when in a most trying and difficult situation.

March 10th.

Poor Captain L. has been censured by the court: but, I have my own opinion. I sincerely pity him; and have wrote to Lord Melville, and Sir Evan Nepean, to try what can be done. All together, I am much unhinged.

To-morrow, if the wind lasts, I shall be off Toulon.

Sir William Bolton is safe, I heard of him this morning. I hear, that a ship is coming out for him; but, as this is only rumour, I cannot keep him from this opportunity of being made post: and, I dare say, he will cause, by his delay, such a tumble, that Louis's son, who I have appointed to the Childers, will lose his promotion; and, then Sir Billy will be wished at the devil! But, I have done with this subject; the whole history has hurt me. Hardy has talked enough to him, to rouze his lethargic disposition.

I have been much hurt at the loss of poor Mr. Girdlestone! He was a good man; but there will be an end of us all.

What has Charles Connor been about? His is a curious letter! If he does not drink, he will do very well. Captain Hilliar has been very good to him.

Colonel Suckling, I find, has sent his son to the Mediterranean; taking him from the Narcissus, where I had been at so much pains to place him. I know not where to find a frigate to place him. He never will be so well and properly situated again. I am more plagued with other people's business, or rather nonsense, than with my own concerns,

With some difficulty, I have got Suckling placed in the Ambuscade, with Captain Durban, who came on board at the moment I was writing.

March 31st.

The history of Suckling will never be done. I have this moment got from him your letter, and one from his father. I shall say nothing to him; I don't blame the child, but those who took [him] out of the most desirable situation in the navy. He never will get into such another advantageous ship: but, his father is a fool; and so, my dear Emma, that *ends*.

The box which you sent me in May 1804, is just arrived in the Diligent store-ship.

I have sent the arms to Palermo, to Gibbs. The clothes are very acceptable; I will give you a kiss, for sending them.

God bless you! Amen.

April 1st.

I am not surprised that we should both think the same about the kitchen; and, if I can afford it, I should like it to be done: but, by the fatal example of poor Mr. Hamilton, and many others, we must take care not to get into debt; for, then, we can neither help any of our relations, and [must] be for ever in misery! But, of this, we [will] talk more, when we walk upon the poop at Merton.

Do you ever see Admiral and Mrs. Lutwidge? You will not forget me when you do.

To Mrs. Cadogan, say every thing that is kind; and to all our other friends: and, be assured, I am, for ever and ever, your's, and only your's,

NELSON & BRONTE.

As I know that all the Mediterranean letters are cut and smoaked, and perhaps read, I do not send you a little letter in this; but your utmost stretch of fancy cannot imagine *more* than I feel towards my own dear Emma.

God bless you! *Amen.*

## LETTER LIX.

Victory, off Plymouth, September 17th, [1805.] Nine o'Clock in the Morning. Blowing fresh at W.S.W. dead foul wind.

I sent, my own Dearest Emma, a letter for you, last night, in a Torbay boat, and gave the man a guinea to put it in the Post-Office.

We have had a nasty blowing night, and it looks very dirty.

I am now signalizing the ships at Plymouth to join me; but, I rather doubt their ability to get to sea. However, I have got clear of Portland, and have Cawsand Bay and Torbay under the lee.

I intreat, my dear Emma, that you will chear up; and we will look forward to many, many happy years, and be surrounded by our children's children. God Almighty can, when he pleases, remove the impediment.

My heart and soul is with you and Horatia.

I got this line ready, in case a boat should get alongside.

For ever, ever, I am your's, most devotedly,

NELSON & BRONTE.

Mr. Rose said, he would write to Mr. Bolton, if I was sailed; but, I have forgot to give him the direction: but I will send it, to-day. I think, I shall succeed very soon, if not at this moment.

Wednesday, September 18th, off the Lizard.

I had no opportunity of sending your letter yesterday, nor do I see any prospect at present. The Ajax and Thunderer are joining; but, it is nearly calm, with a swell from the westward. Perseverance has got us thus far; and the same will, I dare say, get us on.

Thomas seems to do very well, and content.

Tell Mr. Lancaster, that I have no doubt that his son will do very well.

God bless you, my own Emma!

I am giving my letters to Blackwood, to put on board the first vessel he meets going to England, or Ireland.

Once more, Heavens bless you! Ever, for ever, your

NELSON & BRONTE.

## LETTER LX.

Victory, October 1st, 1805.

### MY DEAREST EMMA,

It is a relief to me, to take up the pen, and write you a line; for I have had, about four o'clock this morning, one of my dreadful spasms, which has almost enervated me.

It is very odd! I was hardly ever better than yesterday. Freemantle stayed with me till eight o'clock, and I slept uncommonly well; but, was awoke with this disorder. My opinion of its effect, some one day, has never altered. However, it is entirely gone off, and I am only quite weak. The good people of England will not believe, that rest of body and mind is necessary for me! But, perhaps, this spasm may not come again these six months. I had been writing seven hours yesterday; perhaps, that had some hand in bringing it upon me.

I joined the fleet late on the evening of the 28th of September, but could not communicate with them until the next morning.

I believe, my arrival was most welcome; not only to the commander of the fleet, but also to every individual in it: and, when I came to explain to them the *Nelson touch*, it was like an electric shock. Some shed tears, all approved—"It was new, it was singular, it was simple!" and, from Admirals downwards, it was repeated—"It must succeed, if ever they will allow us to get at them! You are, my Lord, surrounded by friends whom you inspire with confidence." Some may be Judas's; but the majority are certainly much pleased with my commanding them. * * * * * * * * * * * * * * * * * * * * * * *

# SUPPLEMENT.

*INTERESTING LETTERS,*

**ELUCIDATORY**

**OF**

Lord Nelson's Letters

**TO**

**LADY HAMILTON,**

&c.

**VOL. II.**

## LETTERS

**FROM**

**LORD NELSON,**

**TO**

**MISS HORATIA NELSON THOMSON,**

**NOW**

**MISS HORATIA NELSON,**

*(Lord Nelson's Adopted Daughter;)*

**AND**

**MISS CHARLOTTE NELSON,**

*(Daughter of the present Earl.)*

Letters

**OF**

LORD NELSON, &c.

**TO**

**MISS HORATIA NELSON THOMSON.**

Victory, April 13th, 1804.

**MY DEAR HORATIA,**

I send you twelve books of Spanish dresses, which you will let your guardian angel, Lady Hamilton, keep for you, when you are tired of looking at them. I am very glad to hear, that you are perfectly recovered; and, that you are a very good child. I beg, my dear Horatia, that you will always continue so; which will be a great comfort to your most affectionate

NELSON & BRONTE.

## TO MISS CHARLOTTE NELSON.

Victory, April 19th, 1804.

**MY DEAR CHARLOTTE,**

I thank you very much for your kind letters of January 3d, and 4th; and I feel truly sensible of your kind regard for that dear little orphan, Horatia.

Although her parents are lost; yet, she is not without a fortune: and, I shall cherish her to the last moment of my life; and *curse* them who *curse* her, and Heaven *bless* them who *bless* her! Dear innocent! she can have injured no one.

I am glad to hear, that she is attached to you; and, if she takes after her parents, so she will, to those who are kind to her.

I am, ever, dear Charlotte, your affectionate uncle,

NELSON & BRONTE.

## LETTERS

**FROM**

**ALEXANDER DAVISON, ESQ.**

**TO**

**LADY HAMILTON.**

LETTERS OF ALEX. DAVISON, ESQ. &c.

## I.

[1804.]

**MY DEAR MADAM,**

I have, equally with yourself, felt extremely uneasy all night, thinking on *the* letter, which is a very serious one; and, until we receive our next dispatches, I shall still feel every day more and more anxious.

I rely on that kind Providence, which has hitherto sheltered him under every danger, upon the occasion.

He was on the eve of engaging, for protection—and preservation—It is, indeed, an anxious moment!

I have long thought, a plan was in agitation regarding the Toulon fleet being given up; but, whether it was in contemplation at the period the last letter was written, I know not. I am rather disposed to think otherwise.

The next packet will explain the whole; and, I trust, will relieve our minds of that burden, hardly supportable at present.

I shall, this evening, go quietly into the country, and return to town about noon to-morrow: as I require air, and a little relaxation; for I am, actually, overpowered with business.

Your's, most truly,
  ALEX. DAVISON.
Thursday Morning.

## II.

[1804,]

**MY DEAR MADAM,**

Yesterday, I wrote to you just in time to save the post: but, whether that letter, or even this, reach you, I have my doubts—if they do not, you have only yourself to blame; for I cannot, for the soul of me, make out the name of the place. You have been in such a hurry, when writing it, that it really is not legible; and I do not sufficiently know Norfolk, to guess at it.

I did yesterday, as I shall this—imitate your writing, leaving it to the Post-Office gentlemen to find it out.

I acquainted you, that I would take care to obey your wishes, and hold back your check on Coutts and Co. till such time as it would be quite convenient to yourself, and you tell me to send it for payment.

Your mind may be perfectly at ease on that score: as, indeed, it may in every thing in which you have to do with me—though we do, now and then, differ a little in trifles; but, not in essentials: having one, only one, object in mind, that of the comforts, and ultimate happiness, of our dear—*your* beloved Nelson; for whom, what would you or I not do?

What a world of matter is now in agitation! Every thing is big with events; and soon, very soon, I hope to see—what I have long desired, and anxiously [been] waiting for—an event to contribute to the glory, the independency, of our Nelson.

I still hope, ere Christmas, to see him: that hope founded on the darling expectation of his squadron falling in with a rich *Spanish* flotilla. I think, too, that the French fleet will *now* come out.

I have written to our dear friend every information I have been able to collect, and have sent him a continuation of all the newspapers.

It affords me particular pleasure, to hear you feel so happy in Norfolk. How is it possible it can be otherwise! seated, as you are, in the midst of the friends of your best friend; enjoying every kindness and attention in their power to shew to the favourite of their brother.

I shall be very much rejoiced, when you come back, to talk over very interesting objects which our dear friend will *now* have to pursue.

My best respects to your fire-side; and believe me, most sincerely, your's,

**ALEX. DAVISON.**

## III.

Saturday, 22d September 1804.

**MY DEAR MADAM,**

Ever obedient to your *lawful* commands, I have implicitly obeyed your orders, in the purchase, this morning, of Messrs. Branscomb and Co. four quarter lottery-tickets—

{ No. 593.} { 10,376.} { 14,381.} { 20,457.}

Each, I hope, will come up prize; and be entitled to receive, at least, on the whole, twenty thousand pounds! I paid eighteen pounds eight shillings for them; and I have written upon the back of each—"*Property of Lord Nelson, 22d September 1804. A.D.*"

When I have the pleasure of seeing you, I shall deliver the trust over to you, to receive the *bespoken* said sum of twenty thousand pounds. What a glorious receipt will it be!

I am glad you received my letters, though I could not make out the name of the place; the Post-Office runners are expert at it.

What do you say to a Spanish war? I think, now, the breeze begins to freshen; and that the flames, *at last*, will succeed.

I sent off, last night, a very long epistle to our dear Nelson. I am truly distressed at his not receiving my letters; though I can pretty well guess how to account for it, and in whose hands they were detained. Experience teaches us how better to guard against similar misfortunes; and, in future, I shall be cautious to whom I give my letters.

So that I know the Hero of heroes is well, I care the less about letters; knowing that writing, delivering, or receiving them, will not, either in him or me, make the least alteration, or lessen our attachment or affection.

I am pleased to see how happy you are in Norfolk. I wish you may not find it so fascinating, that the arrival of "Lord Nelson" at Merton would not induce you to [quit] the county!!!

I beg you will make my best respects acceptable to *every* friend (real) of that invaluable man, Lord Nelson.

    Your's, most truly,
    ALEX. DAVISON.

Letter

from

Lady Hamilton

**TO**

**ALEXANDER DAVISON, ESQ.**

**INCLOSING**

*Her Ladyship's Verses on Lord Nelson.*

Letter OF Lady Hamilton, &c.

Clarges                                                   Street,
*[26th January 1805.]*

I have been very ill, my Dear Sir; and am in bed with a cold, very bad cold indeed! But, the moment I am better, I will call on you.

I am invited to dine with Mr. Haslewood to-morrow, but fear I shall not be able to go.

I am very anxious about letters; but Admiral Campbell has told me, he thinks my dear Lord will soon be at home. God grant! for, I think, he might remove that stumbling-block, Sir John O! Devil take him!

That *Polyphemus* should have been Nelson's: but, he is rich in great and *noble deeds*; which t'other, poor devil! is not. So, let dirty wretches get pelf, to comfort them; victory belongs to Nelson. Not, but what I think money necessary for comforts; and, I hope, *our, your's,* and *my* Nelson, will get a little, for all Master O.

I write from bed; and you will see I do, by my scrawl.

I send you some of my bad Verses on my soul's Idol.

God bless you! Remember, you will soon be free; and let that cheer you, that you will come out with even more friends than ever. I can only say, I am your ever obliged, and grateful,

**EMMA HAMILTON.**

I long to see and know Nepean! Why will you not ask me to dine with, him *en famille?*

> {Yes.}
> {*A.D.*}

\* \* \* \* \*

**EMMA TO NELSON.**

I think, I have not lost my heart;
  Since I, with truth, can swear,
At every moment of my life,
  I feel my Nelson there!

If, from thine Emma's breast, her heart
  Were stolen or flown away;
Where! where! should she my Nelson's love
  Record, each happy day?

If, from thine Emma's breast, her heart
  Were stolen or flown away;
Where! where! should she engrave, my Love!
  Each tender word you say?

Where! where! should Emma treasure up
  Her Nelson's smiles and sighs?
Where mark, with joy, each secret look
  Of love, from Nelson's eyes?

Then, do not rob me of my heart,
  Unless you first forsake it;
And, then, so wretched it would be,
  Despair alone will take it.

Letter

from

Lady Hamilton

## TO THE

## RIGHT HONOURABLE HENRY ADDINGTON,

## NOW

## VISCOUNT SIDMOUTH.

Letter of Lady Hamilton, &c.

April 13th. [1803.]

## SIR,

May I trouble you, and but for a moment, in consequence of my irreparable loss; my ever-honoured husband, Sir William Hamilton, being no more! I cannot avoid it, I am forced to petition for a portion of his pension: such a portion as, in your wisdom and noble nature, may be approved; and so represented to our most gracious Sovereign, as being right. For, Sir, I am most sadly bereaved! I am now in circumstances far below those in which the goodness of my dear Sir William allowed me to move for so many years; and below those becoming the relict of such a public minister, who was proved so very long—no less than thirty-six years—and, all his life, honoured so very much by the constant friendly kindness of the King and Queen themselves: and, may I mention—what is well known to the then administration at home—how I, too, strove to do all I could towards the service of our King and Country. The fleet itself, I can truly say, could not have got into *Sicily*, but for what I was happily able to do with the Queen of Naples, and through her secret instructions so obtained: on which depended the refitting of the fleet in Sicily; and, with that, all which followed so gloriously at the Nile. These few words, though seemingly much at large, may not be extravagant at all. They are, indeed, true. I wish them to be heard, only as they can be proved; and, being proved, may I hope for what I have now desired?

I am, Sir, with respect more than I can well utter, your obedient servant,

## EMMA HAMILTON.

Letters

## FROM

## SIR WILLIAM HAMILTON, K.B.

## TO

## LADY HAMILTON.

## I.

Persano,                                                          [Wednesday]
Jan. 4, 1792.

We arrived here, yesterday, in little more than five hours, and had nearly began with a disagreeable accident; for the King's horse took fright at the guard, and his Majesty and horse were as near down as possible. However, all ended well; and he was as gay as possible, yesterday.

Our first *chasse* has not succeeded; though there were two wolves, and many wild boars, in the *Mena*: but the king would direct how we should beat the wood, and began at the wrong end; by which the wolves and boars escaped, and we remained without shooting power. However, ten or twelve boars have been killed, some how or other, and some large ones.

The King's face is very long, at this moment; but, I dare say, to-morrow's good sport will shorten it again.

I was sorry, my dear Em. to leave you in affliction: you must harden yourself to such little misfortunes as a temporary parting; but, I cannot blame you for having a good and tender heart. Believe me, you are in thorough possession of all mine, though I will allow it to be rather tough.

Let us study to make one another as comfortable as we can; and "*banish sorrow, till to-morrow.*" and so on, every day.

You are wise enough to see the line it is proper for you to take; and have, hitherto, followed it most rigorously: and I can assure you, that I have not the least doubt of your continuing in it.

Amuse yourself as well as you can, as I am doing, whilst we are separate; and the best news you can give me is, that you are well and happy.

My cold is already better for having passed the whole day in the open air, and without human *seccatura*.

Adieu! my dear, dear Emma. I am, with my love to your good mother, your's ever, and faithfully,

**W.H.**

# II.

Persano, Thursday,
[Jan. 5th, 1792.]

We got home early, and I have not yet received your Daily Advertiser.

No sport, again! In the midst of such a quantity of game, they have contrived to carry him far off, where there is none. He has no other comfort, to-day, than having killed a wild cat; and his face is a yard long.

However, his Majesty has vowed vengeance on the boars to-morrow, and will go according to his own fancy; and, I dare say, there will be a terrible slaughter.

The last day, we are to keep all we kill; and, I suppose, it will be night before we get home.

Yesterday, the courier brought the order of St. Stephano, from the Emperor, for the Prince Ausberg, and the King was desired to invest him with it. As soon as the King received it, he ran into the Prince's room; whom he found in his shirt, and without his breeches: and, in that condition, was he decorated with the star and ribbon by his Majesty, who has wrote the whole circumstance to the Emperor.

Leopold may, perhaps, not like the joking with his first order. Such nonsense should, certainly, be done with solemnity; or it becomes, what it really is, a little tinsel, and a few yards of broad ribbon.

The Prince, *entre nous*, is not very wise; but he is a good creature and we are great friends.

I have wrote to Mrs. Dickinson. I forget whether you have, or not: if not, pray do it soon; for, you know, she is a good friend of your's.

I have just received your good letter. I am glad they have taken the Guarda patana's son-in-law. I insist upon Smith's letting the Regent of the Vicaria know of his having stabbed my porter. He ought to go to the gallies; and my honour is concerned, if this insult offered my livery is unnoticed. The girl had better cry, than be ill-used, and her father killed.

Adieu, my sweet Em. Your's, with all my heart,

**W.H.**

# III.

Persano, Friday Evening.
[Jan. 6th, 1792.]

I Inclose our friend Knight's admirable letter to you. I could not refrain reading it; and, I am sure, it was his intention I should do so, having left it unsealed. He is a fine fellow; it was worth going to England, to secure such a sensible friend.

You will probably have seen General Werner last night; this is Friday night, and he will have told you I am well.

We have been out all day in the rain; I killed none, and the King and party but few. Such obstinate bad weather I really never experienced, for so long a time together.

You did perfectly right in buying the lamps; and I am glad the Prince asked to dine with you. I am sure, he was comfortably received by you.

You see what devils [there are] in England! They wanted to stir up something against me; but our conduct shall be such as to be unattackable: and I fear not an injustice from England. Twenty-seven years service— having spent all the King's money, and all my own, besides running in debt, deserves something better than a dismission!

The King has declared, he will return to Naples next Saturday se'n-night; so you know the worst, my dear Emma. Indeed, I shall embrace you most cordially; for I would not be married to any woman, but yourself, on earth, for all the world.

Lord A. Hamilton's son, you see, recommends a friend of his; who, I suppose, is arrived: if so, receive him well.

Adieu, again! Your's, ever,

**W.H.**

# IV.

Persano, Saturday Night,
[January 7th, 1792.]

This has been one of the cruel days which attend the King's *chasse*. All the posts—except the King's, Prince Ausberg, D'Onerato, and Priori—bad.

We have been out all day, in cold rain, without seeing a boar. The King has killed twenty-five, and a wolf; and the other good posts, in proportion.

Why not rather leave us at home, than go out with the impossibility of sport? But we must take the good and bad, or give it up.

Lamberg is too delicate for this business; he has been in bed, with a slight fever, all to-day.

You will have another boar, to-day; which boar being a *sow*, I have made a *bull!* The sows are much better than the boars; so you may keep some to eat at home, and dispose of the rest to your favourite English.

I am glad all goes on so well. I never doubted your gaining every soul you approach.

I am far from being angry at your feeling the loss of me so much! Nay, I am flattered; but, believe me, the time will soon come, that we shall meet. Years pass seemingly in an instant; why, then, afraid of a few days?

Upon the whole, we are sociable here; but we go to bed at nine, and get up at five o'clock. I generally read an hour, to digest my supper; but, indeed, I live chiefly on bread and butter.

Salandra desires his compliments to you, as does Lamberg and Prince Ausberg.

Adieu, my dear Emma! Ever your's, and your's alone,

**W.H.**

I send you back your two letters. Dutens was very satisfactory. I send the papers to Smith; who will give them to you first, if you have not read them.

The cold and fatigue makes my hand something like your's—which, by the bye, you neglect rather too much: but, as what you write is good sense, every body will forgive the scrawl.

## V.

Sunday Night, [Jan. 8th, 1792.]

We are come in late; and I have but a moment to tell you we are well, and I have killed three large boars, a fox, and four woodcocks.

Nothing pleases me more, than to hear you do not neglect your singing. It would be a pity, as you are near the point of perfection.

Adieu, my dearest Emma! Your's, with my whole soul,

**W.H.**

# VI.

Persano, [Monday]
January 10th, [9th] 1792.

Your letter of yesterday, my Sweet Em. gave me great pleasure; as, I see, all goes on perfectly right for you at Naples.

Your business, and mine, is to be civil to all, and not enter into any party matters. If the Wilkinsons are not content with our civilities, let them help themselves.

We have had a charming day, and most excellent sport. More than a hundred wild boars, and two wolves, have fallen. I killed five boars, truly monsters! and a fox.

Vincenzo could not follow me to-day; he cannot walk two steps, without being out of breath. However, I load the guns myself; and, with the peasant I brought from Caserta, and another I hire here, I do very well. I fear, poor Vincenzo will not hold long. If he chooses it, I mean to send him to Naples, to consult Noody [Nudi.]

General Werner, Prince of Hesse, and Count Zichare, are here since last night; they brought me your compliments. Lamberg is still confined.

Amuse yourself, my dearest Emma, and never doubt of my love. Your's, ever,

**W.H.**

# VII.

Persano, [Tuesday]
Jan. 10th, 1792.

The day has been so thoroughly bad, that we have not been able to stir out; and the King, of course, in bad humour. I am not sorry to have a day's repose, and I have wrote my letters for to-morrow's post.

Lamberg is still in bed with a fever, and Prince Ausberg's eyes are a little inflamed with cold and fatigue. My cold was renewed a little yesterday; but a good night's rest, and quiet to-day, has set all to rights again.

Vincenzo was so bad, yesterday, that he could not follow me, and was blooded. He is better, to-day; but he will never serve more, except to load my guns at the post. He cannot walk a mile, without being out of breath.

I am glad you have been at the Academy, and in the great world. It is time enough for you to find out, that the only real comfort is to be met with at home; I have been in that secret some time.

You are, certainly, the most domestic young woman I know: but you are young, and most beautiful; and it would not be natural, if you did not like to shew yourself a little in public.

The effusion of tenderness, with regard to me, in your letter, is very flattering; I know the value of it, and will do all I can to keep it alive. We are now one flesh, and it must be our study to keep that flesh as warm and comfortable as we can. I will do all in my power to please you, and I do not doubt of your doing the same towards me.

Adieu, my dearest Emma! Having nothing interesting to write, and as you insist upon hearing from me every day, you must content yourself with such a stupid letter as this.

Your Ladyship's commands shall always be punctually obeyed by, dear Madam, your Ladyship's most obedient and faithful servant,

**W. HAMILTON.**

## VIII.

Persano, Wednesday,
11th Jan. [1792.]

I have just received your letter—and, as I always do—with infinite pleasure.

I hope you received twelve wood-biddies, to-day; and, to-morrow, you will have a wild boar: all left to your discretion.

No talk of returning, yet. We must complete sixteen days shooting, and one day has been lost by bad weather.

We had a good day, and tolerable sport. I have killed two, and one the largest boar I have seen yet here.

Vincenzo, they say, will be well in a day or two, as it is only a cold; I fear, it is more serious.

The King has killed twenty-one boars to-day, and is quite happy.

The Germans all drink tea with me every evening. Lamberg is better.

Adieu, my ever dear Emma! We are always in a hurry; though we have, absolutely, nothing to do, but kill, examine, and weigh, wild boars.

I assure you, that I shall rejoice when I can embrace you once more. A picture would not content me; your image is more strongly represented on my heart, than any that could be produced by human art.

Your most affectionate husband,

**W.H.**

## IX.

Persano, Thursday Night,
[Jan. 12th, 1792.]

Never put yourself in a hurry, my dear Emma.

I have got your two kind letters. Send for Gasparo; and give your orders, that the servants attend your call: and let him discharge them, if they do not. You are my better half, and may command. Translate this part of the letter to him.

We have had good sport to-day, though the bad weather came on at eleven o'clock. Fifty-four wild boars have been killed, I had seven shot; and killed five, three of which are enormous. Dispose of the boar I send you to-day as you think proper.

I always thought Ruspoli a dirty fellow; but what has he done of late?

As to your mother's going with you to the English parties, very well; but, believe me, it will be best for her, and more to her happiness, to stay at home, than go with you to the Neapolitan parties.

The King is in good humour to-day, as I foretold. We continue to dine at eight at night, and have nothing from breakfast to that hour. But I give tea and bread and butter, of which Prince Ausberg and Lamberg partake with pleasure. The Prince, having no opportunity of making love, does nothing but talk of his new flame, which is Lady A. Hatton. I put him right; for he thought she spelt her name with two *rr*, instead of two *tt*.

I rejoice at your having Aprile again; pray, tell him so: for I know the rapid progress you will make under his care.

My cold is near gone. The worst is, my room smokes confoundedly; and so do all the other rooms, except the King's.

Adieu, my dear Emma! Amuse yourself as well as you can; and believe me, ever, your's alone, with the utmost confidence,

**W.H.**

# X.

Persano, Friday Night,
[Jan. 13th, 1792.]

We have had a miserable cold day, but good sport. I killed two boars, and a doe; the King, nineteen boars, two stags, two does, and a porcupine. He is happy beyond expression.

I send you Charles's letter; but do not lose it, as I will answer it when I return. You see, the line we have taken will put it out of the power of our enemies to hurt us. I will give up my judgment of worldly matters to no one.

I approve of all you do in my absence; but it would be nonsense, and appear affected, to carry your scruples too far. Divert yourself reasonably. I am sure of your attachment to me, and I shall not easily be made to alter my opinion of you.

My cold is better, notwithstanding the weather.

I have no time to *in'gler*; so, adieu! my dearest wife.

Your's,

**W.H.**

*P.S.* Let Gasparo pay thirty ducats, for the vase, to D. Andrea.

By way of charity, we may give thirty ounces to that shabby dog, Hadrava; though he knows the picture is not worth more than ten at most. His writing to you in such a stile is pitiful indeed. You will often have such letters, if you do not tell him, now, that it is for once and all.

# XI.

Persano, Saturday, 14th Jan. [1792.]

**MY DEAR EMMA,**

I have received a letter from Douglass; with one inclosed, from Mr. Durno; who, to my surprise, says, he has not received my order on Biddulph, Cockes, and Co. for one thousand five hundred and ninety pounds; which, you know, I sent from Caserta.

I find, in my book of letters, 20th of December, that I wrote, that day, a letter to Mr. Burgess, to deliver to Messieurs Biddulph and Co.—to Lord Abercorn—and to Mr. Durno, with the order inclosed.

Pray, send for Smith; and ask him, if he remembers having put such letters in the post, and let him inquire at the Naples post about them: and let him send the inclosed, by Tuesday's post, to Rome.

I certainly will not give another order until this matter is cleared up. I fear some roguery.

We have had a fine day, and killed numberless boars; a hundred and fifty, at least. I have killed four, out of six shot; and am satisfied, as one is a real monster—the King, thirty—D'Onerato, eighteen,—and so on, the favoured shooters.

Vincenzo is rather better, but not able to serve me.

My best compliments to Alexander Hamilton. You did well, to invite Copley.

Adieu! my sweet Em. Ever your's, in deed and in truth,

**W.H.**

## XII.

Persano, Sunday,
Jan. 15, 1792.

You did admirably, my Dear Em. in not inviting Lady A.H. to dine with the Prince; and still better, in telling her, honestly, the reason. I have always found, that going straight is the best method, though not the way of the world.

You did, also, very well, in asking Madame Skamouski; and not taking upon you to present her, without leave.

In short, consult your own good sense, and do not be in a hurry; and, I am sure, you will always act right.

We have been at it again, this morning, and killed fifty boars; but were home to dinner, at one o'clock: and this is the first dinner I have had, since I left you; for I cannot eat meat breakfasts or suppers, and have absolutely lived on bread and butter and tea.

As the Prince asked you, you did well to send for a song to Douglass's; but, in general, you will do right to sing only at home.

The King is very kind to me, and shews every one that he really loves me: and he commends my shooting; having missed but very few, and killed the largest of the society. Only think of his not being satisfied with killing more than thirty, yesterday! He said, if the wind had favoured him, he should have killed sixty at least.

We must be civil to Mr. Hope, as recommended by Lord Auckland; and also to Monsieur de Rochement, and Prince Bozatinsky, as recommended by my friend Saussure. I inclose his letter, as you are mentioned in it; also Knight's, as you desire. God knows, we have no secrets; nor, I hope, ever shall.

We have much business between this and Saturday: and we are to shoot, Saturday morning; so that we shall arrive late.

What say you to a feet washing that night? *O che Gusto!* when your *prima ora* is over, and all gone.

Adieu, my sweet Emma! Ever your's,

**W.H.**

## XIII.

Persano, Monday Night,
[Jan. 16th, 1792.]

For your long and interesting letter, I can only write a line, to tell you I am well.

We have been out, till an hour in the night, from day-break; and I have fired off my gun but once, having had a bad post. The King, and favoured party, have diverted themselves. To-morrow will, probably, be a good day for me.

Pray, let Smith get orders for the Museum, &c. for Lord Boyle and Mr. Dodge, as they are recommended by Mr. Eden.

Adieu, my lovely Emma! Let them all roll on the carpet, &c. provided you are not of the party. My trust is in you alone.

Your's, ever,

**W.H.**

# XIV.

Persano, Tuesday Night,
[Jan. 17, 1792.]

I told you, my Dear Em. that I expected good sport to-day! I have killed five boars, and two great ones got off after falling; two bucks; six does; and a hare: fourteen in all.

By the bye, I must tell you, that *accept* and *except* are totally different. You always write—"I did not *except* of the invitation;" when, you know, it should be "*accept*." It is, only, for want of giving yourself time to think; but, as this error has been repeated, I thought best to tell you of it.

Pray, write a very kind letter to our friend the Archbishop; and convince him, that Emma, to her friends, is unalterable. Do not say a word about the telescope; for, I must try it, first, against mine. If it should be better, I cannot part with it, as you know how much use we make of a telescope.

The King has killed eighty-one animals, of one sort or other, to-day; and, amongst them, a wolf, and some stags. He fell asleep in the coach; and, waking, told me he had been dreaming of shooting. One would have thought, he had shed blood enough.

This is a heavy air; nobody eats with appetite, and many are ill with colds.

We shall be home on Saturday; and, indeed, my sweet Emma, I shall be most happy to see you.

To-morrow, we go to a mountain; but no great expectation of sport.

Your's, ever, my dear wife,

**W.H.**

# XV.

Persano, Wednesday,
[Jan. 18th, 1792.]

It was not your white and silver, alone, that made you look like an angel, at the Academy. Suppose you had put it on nine parts out of ten of the ladies in company, would any one have appeared angelic?

I will allow, however, that a beautiful woman, feeling herself well dressed, will have a sort of confidence, which will add greatly to the lustre of her eye: but take my word, that, for some years to come, the more simply you dress, the more conspicuous will be your beauty; which, according to my idea, is the most perfect I have yet met with, take it all in all.

It is long-faced day with the King. We went far; the weather was bad; and, after all, met with little or no game: I did not fire off my gun.

Yesterday, when we brought home all we killed, it filled the house, completely; and, to-day, they are obliged to white-wash the walls, to take away the blood. There were more than four hundred; boars, deer, stags, and all.

To-morrow, we are to have another slaughter; and not a word of reason or common sense do I meet with, the whole day, till I retire to my volumes of the old Gentleman's Magazine, which just keeps my mind from starving.

Except to-day, on a mountain, I have never felt the least appetite; there, I eat the wings of a cold chicken with pleasure.

Hamilton is delighted with your civilities. He has wrote me a long letter. I do not mean to keep pace with him in writing; so, send him a line or two, only, in answer.

I do not recollect the name of Marino Soolania; and, if I received a letter from him, it was in the hurry of my arrival, and is lost: so that Smith may desire the Dutch Consul to desire him to write again, and I will answer.

I always rejoice when I find you do not neglect your singing. I am, I own, ambitious of producing something extraordinary in you, and it is nearly done.

Adieu! my sweet Em. I rejoice that the time of our re-union is so near— *Saturday night!*

**W.H.**

## XVI.

Venasso, Friday, 27th January 1794.

**MY DEAR EM.**

By having grumbled a little, I got a better post to-day; and have killed two boars and a sow, all enormous. I have missed but two shot since I came here; and, to be sure, when the post is good, it is noble shooting! The rocks, and mountains, as wild as the boars.

The news you sent me, of poor Lord Pembroke, gave me a little twist; but I have, for some time, perceived, that my friends, with whom I spent my younger days, have been dropping around me.

Lord Pembroke's neck was very short, and his father died of an apoplexy.

My study of antiquities, has kept me in constant thought of the perpetual fluctuation of every thing. The whole art is, really, to live all the *days* of our life; and not, with anxious care, disturb the sweetest hour that life affords— which is, the present! Admire the Creator, and all his works, to us incomprehensible: and do all the good you can upon earth; and take the chance of eternity, without dismay.

You must tell the Archbishop, that he will have the Leyden gazettes a week later; as I cannot read them time enough to send by this messenger.

The weather is delightful; and, I believe, we shall have done all our business, so as to return on Thursday.

Pray, find out if the Queen goes to Caserta. Here, all is a profound secret.

I must work hard, myself, at translating, when I return; for I believe the language-master totally incapable of it.

I dined, this morning, at nine o'clock; and, I think, it agreed better with me than tea. I found myself growing weak, for want of a good meal, not daring to eat much at supper.

Adieu, my sweet love! adieu. Divert yourself—I shall soon be at you again. Your's, ever,

**W.H.**

## XVII.

Burford, Eighty Miles from London.
Saturday Night, [July 27th, 1801.]

Here we are, my Dear Emma, after a pleasant day's journey! No extraordinary occurrence. Our chaise is good, and would have held the famous "*Tria juncta in Uno*," very well: but, we must submit to the circumstances of the times.

Sir Joseph Bankes we found in bed with the gout: and, last night, his hot-house was robbed of its choicest fruit—peaches and nectarines.

Amuse yourself as well as you can; and you may be assured, that I shall return as soon as possible, and you shall hear from me often.

Ever your's, my dear Emma, with the truest affection,

Wm. HAMILTON.

My kindest love to my Lord, if he is not gone.

*P.S.* Corn, at this market, fell fifteen pounds a load to-day.

Letters

# FROM

# SIR WILLIAM HAMILTON, K.B.

# TO

# LORD NELSON.

Letters OF SIR WILLIAM HAMILTON, K.B. &c.

# I.

*[Written before LORD NELSON'S Elevation to the Peerage.]*

Naples, March 26th, 1796.

## MY DEAR SIR,

The moment I received your letter of the 11th of March from Leghorn, I went with it to General Acton: and, although I could not, from your letter only, in my Ministerial character, demand from this Court the assistance of some of their xebecs, corvettes, &c. that are the fittest for going near shore; as I think, with you, that such vessels are absolutely necessary on the present occasion, I told his Excellency—that I trusted, as this government had hitherto shewn itself as sanguine in the good cause, and more so, than any of the allies of Great Britain, that he would lay your letter before the King at Naples; and, without waiting for the demand which I should probably receive soon from Sir John Jervis, send you such small armed vessels as his Excellency thought would be proper for the service on which you are employed.

The General, without hesitation, said—that orders should be immediately given for the preparing of such a flotilla, which should join you as soon as the weather would permit. At present, indeed, it is not very encouraging for row-boats.

We wait a courier from Vienna, to decide the march of eight thousand eight hundred infantry, and artillery included, intended to join the Emperor's army in Italy: and, although the Grand Duke of Tuscany has refused the permission for these troops to march through his dominions, the King of Naples has told his son-in-law that, whenever the safety of Italy should require it, he would, nevertheless, march them through Tuscany; a liberty which the Emperor would likewise take, whenever the good of the service required it.

However, the thousand cavalry sent from hence have taken their route, by Loretto, through the Pope's state.

We have had, as I suppose you know, the Admirals Hotham and Goodall here, for some weeks. I can, *entre nous*, perceive that my old friend Hotham is not quite awake enough for such a command as that of the King's fleet in the Mediterranean, although he appears the best creature imaginable.

I did not know much of your friend Lord Hood, personally; but, by his correspondence with me, his activity and clearness was most conspicuous.

Lady Hamilton and I admire your constancy, and hope the severe service you have undergone will be handsomely rewarded.

When I reported to Lord Grenville, in my last dispatch, the letter I received from you lately, I could not help giving you the epithet of "*that brave officer, Captain Nelson.*" If you do not deserve it, I know not who does.

With our love to Sam, I am, ever, dear Sir, your's, sincerely,

Wm. HAMILTON.

## II.

Palermo, February 13th, 1799.

**MY LORD,**

Having received an application from this government, that they might be supplied with lead from on board the British merchants ships in this harbour, that have that article on board—and that, without the help of about a hundred *cantarra* of lead, this country, and the common cause, would be much distressed—I am to beg of your Lordship to use your kind endeavours that this urgent want may be supplied as soon as possible: well understood, that the proprietors of this article should be perfectly satisfied with this government, as to the price of the lead, freight, &c.

I have the honour to be, my Lord, your Lordship's most obedient and most humble servant,

Wm. HAMILTON.

## III.

Palermo, Sunday Night late, near winding-up-watch hour, May 19th, 1799.

**MY VERY DEAR LORD,**

Ten thousand thanks for your kind attention in sending us Hallowell's letter to Troubridge. It comforts us in one respect, as it flatters us with Commodore Duckworth's four ships joining you soon. But, I must own, from the junction of five Spanish ships and frigates, I now think, something more than going into Toulon is intended, and that your Lordship may have a brush with them.

God send you every success, that your unparalleled virtues and bravery so well merit.

Adieu, my dear Lord! Your Lordship's truly affectionate, and eternally attached,

Wm. HAMILTON.

## IV.

Palermo, May 26th, 1799.

**MY DEAR LORD,**

Whilst Emma was writing to your Lordship, I have been with Acton, to get a felucca, to send Ball's dispatch to you. It is of so old a date, that I make no doubt of Ball's having joined you before his dispatch reaches.

I send your Lordship an interesting letter I have just received from our Consul at Trieste: and Acton's answer to my yesterday's letter communicating your kind resolution of taking care of their Sicilian Majesties and their kingdoms; and which, your Lordship will see, gives them great satisfaction.

As to the fleet having been seen by the Towers near Messina, and to the westward—I believe, it was your squadron.

I send you, likewise, a strange rhapsody from Lord Bristol: but something may be collected from it; or, at least, it will amuse you, and you have leisure enough on board, which I have not on shore. Be so good as to send back that letter, and Graham's, by the first opportunity.

Above all, take care of your health; that is the first of blessings. May God ever protect you! We miss you heavily: but, a short time must clear up the business; and, we hope, bring you back to those who love and esteem you to the very bottom of their souls.

Ever your affectionate friend, and humble servant,

Wm. HAMILTON.

# V.

Palermo, June 17th, 1799.

**MY DEAR LORD,**

I am happy to receive the packet from Major Magra, and which I shall instantly send to General Acton.

Nothing has happened, worth telling you, since the few hours we have been separated.

God bless you, my very dear friend; and my mind tells me, that you will soon have reason, either by good news, or by a proper reinforcement sent to you, to be in a much happier state of mind than you could possibly be when you left us this morning. All looks melancholy without you.

Ever, my dear Lord, your truly attached friend,

Wm. HAMILTON.

# VI.

Palermo, June 20th, 1799.
Eight o'Clock at Night.

**MY DEAR LORD,**

Having wrote fully by the felucca to-day, that went off at three o'clock—and have not yet General Acton's answer, with respect to what the Court would wish you to do when you hear how the French fleet is disposed of—I have nothing to write by the transport.

God bless you! And I hope, somehow or other, we shall meet again soon.

My dear Lord, your's, most sincerely,

Wm. HAMILTON.

# VII.

Piccadilly, February 19th, 1801.

**MY DEAR LORD,**

Whether Emma will be able to write to you to-day, or not, is a question; as she has got one of her terrible sick head-achs. Among other things that vex her, is—that we have been drawn in to be under the absolute necessity of giving a dinner to ****** on Sunday next. He asked it himself; having expressed his strong desire of hearing Banti's and Emma's voices together.

I am well aware of the danger that would attend ******* frequenting our house. Not that I fear, that Emma could ever be induced to act contrary to the prudent conduct she has hitherto pursued; but the world is so ill-natured, that the worst construction is put upon the most innocent actions.

As this dinner must be, or ****** would be offended, I shall keep it strictly to the musical part; invite only Banti, her husband, and Taylor; and, as I wish to shew a civility to Davison, I have sent him an invitation.

In short, we will get rid of it as well as we can, and guard against its producing more meetings of the same sort.

Emma would really have gone any lengths, to have avoided Sunday's dinner. But I thought it would not be prudent to break with ******; who, really, has shewn the greatest civility to us, when we were last in England, and since we returned: and she has, at last, acquiesced to my opinion.

I have been thus explicit, as I know well your Lordship's way of thinking; and your very kind attachment to us, and to every thing that concerns us.

The King caught cold at the Chapel the other day, and there was no levee yesterday; and, to-day, the Queen alone will be at the drawing-room: and, I believe, the new ministry will not be quite fixed, until the levee-day next week.

As to my business—I have done all I can to bring it to a point.

The pension recommended by Lord Grenville was only like Walpole's—a nominal two thousand pounds. I have represented the injustice of that—after my having had the King's promise of not being removed from Naples, but at my own request; and having only empowered Lord Grenville to remove me, on securing to me a nett income of two thousand pounds per annum.

Lord Grenville has recommended to the Treasury, the taking my extraordinary expences into consideration.

I have fully demonstrated, to Lord Grenville and Treasury, that eight thousand pounds is absolutely necessary for the clearing off my unfunded debt, without making up for my losses.

Upon the whole, then, I do not expect to get more than the nett annuity above mentioned, and the eight thousand pounds. But, unless that is granted, I shall, indeed, have been very ill-used! I hope, in my next, to be able to inform your Lordship that all has been finally settled.

I am busy in putting in order the remains of my vases and pictures, that you so kindly saved for me on board the Fourdroyant; and the sale of them will enable me to go on more at my ease, and not leave a debt unpaid. But, unfortunately, there have been too many picture sales this year, and mine will come late.

Adieu! my very dear Lord. May health and success attend you, wherever you go! And, I flatter myself, this political jumble may hasten a peace, and bring you back soon.

Your Lordship's ever obliged, and most sincerely attached, friend and servant,

Wm. HAMILTON.

## VIII.

Piccadilly, February 20th, 1801.

**MY DEAR LORD,**

You need not be the least alarmed, that Emma has commissioned me to send you the newspapers; and write you a line, to tell you that she is much better—having vomited naturally, and is now purposing to take a regular one of tartar emetic.

All her convulsive complaints certainly proceed from a foul stomach; and I will answer for it, she will be in spirits to write to you herself to-morrow.

Adieu! my very dear Lord. I have not a moment to lose, as the bell is going.

Your ever attached and obliged humble servant,

Wm. HAMILTON.

## IX.

Piccadilly, March 7th, 1801.

**MY VERY DEAR LORD,**

I wish it was in my power to profit of your kind invitation; you would soon see me and Emma on board the St. George: but I am now totally occupied in preparing for the sale of my pictures, and what I have saved of my vases.

To my great satisfaction, I have found some of the most capital vases; and which I thought, surely, lost on board the Colossus. It has comforted me much.

We remain in the same cruel state with respect to the King's recovery. There can be no doubt, but that his Majesty is better. However, if my conjectures are true, the Regency must soon take place: as it may be long before his Majesty could be troubled with business, supposing even his *fever* to have totally subsided; and, the times admit of no delays.

We see, now, the certainty of the French squadron's being in the Mediterranean. God knows, how all this will end! But I hope it will be your Lordship's lot to bring Paul to his senses.

God send you every success; and send you home, safe and well, crowned with additional laurels! And then, I hope, you will repose your shattered frame; and make your friends happy, by staying with them.

Emma

Emma is certainly much better, but not quite free from bile.

Ever, my dear Lord, your Lordship's most attached, and eternally obliged, humble servant,

Wm. HAMILTON.

## X.

Piccadilly, April 16th, 1801.

What can I say, my Dear Lord! that would convey the smallest idea of what we felt yesterday, on receiving the authentic letters confirming your late most glorious victory: and read, in your own hand, that God had not only granted you complete success against the enemies of our country; but, in the midst of such perils, prevented your receiving the smallest scratch!

We can only repeat what we knew well, and often said, before—that Nelson *was*, *is*, and to the *last* will ever be, *the first*.

However, we all agree that, when we get you safe home once more—that you should never more risk your shattered frame.

You have done enough, and are well entitled to the motto of Virgil—

"*Hic Victor cæstus artemque repono.*"

The famous Broughton, after he had beaten every opponent, that dared to measure hard blows with him, set up an ale-house—the Broughton's Head—in London, with the above verse of Virgil under it. Some years after, he was persuaded to accept the challenge of a coachman, and was beaten.

Not that I mean to convey, that any such thing could happen to your Lordship; but, you have done enough. Let others follow your examples; they will be remembered to the latest posterity.

It appeared to me most extraordinary, that the 6th inst. the date of your last letter to Emma, the death of the Emperor Paul (which we have no doubt of here) should not be known at Copenhagen!

It appears to us that, as soon as that great event is known in Sweden and Denmark, with the severe blow you have just given the latter, the formidable giant, Northern Coalition, will of itself fall to pieces; and that we shall have the happiness of embracing you again here, in a very short time.

You would have laughed to have seen what I saw yesterday! *Emma* did not know whether she was on her head or heels—in such a hurry to tell your great news, that she could utter nothing but tears of joy and tenderness.

I went to Davison yesterday morning; and found him still in bed, having had a severe fit of the gout, and with your letter, which he had just received: and he cried like a child! But, what was very extraordinary, assured me that, from the instant he had read your letter, all pain had left him, and that he felt himself able to get up and walk about.

Your brother, Mrs. Nelson, and Horace, dined with us. Your brother was more extraordinary than ever. He would get up suddenly, and cut a caper; rubbing his hands every time that the thought of your fresh laurels came into his head.

In short, except myself, (and your Lordship knows that I have some phlegm) all the company, which was considerable, after dinner—the Duke, Lord William, Mr. Este, &c.—were mad with joy. But, I am sure, that no one really rejoiced more, at heart, than I did. I have lived too long to have *extacies!* But, with calm reflection, I felt for my friend having got to the very summit of glory!—the "*Ne plus ultra!*"—that he has had another opportunity of rendering his country the most important service; and manifesting, again, his judgment, his intrepidity, and humanity.

God bless you, my very dear Lord, and send you soon home to your friends. Enemies you have none, but those that are bursting with envy; and such animals infest all parts of the world.

The King, be assured, is (though weak) getting well fast. Lord Loughborough told Livingston, who has just been here, that he was with the King the day before yesterday, before and after delivery of the seals, and that he was perfectly calm and recollected.

Ever your sincerely attached, and truly obliged, humble servant,

Wm. HAMILTON.

# XI.

Milford, August 12th, 1801.

**MY DEAR LORD,**

Emma has constantly given me every possible intelligence relative to your Lordship, and the important operations you are about at this most interesting moment.

You have already calmed the minds of every body with respect to the threatened French invasion. In short, all your Lordship does is complete; like yourself, and nobody else. But still, I think, there is no occasion for the Commander in Chief to expose his person as much as you do. Why should you not have a private flag, known to your fleet and not to the enemy, when you shift it and go reconnoitring?

Captain Hopkins, going from hence in the Speedwell cutter to join your Lordship, will be happy to introduce himself to you by presenting this letter himself. They give him a good character in this country, but my acquaintance with him is but of two days.

I was yesterday with Captain Dobbins, in the Diligence cutter. We sailed out of this glorious harbour; and, the day being fine, sailed out some leagues, and examined the Crow Rock, which is reckoned the greatest danger as to entering the harbour. But the two light-houses lately erected take off all danger in the night; and [it] is visible in the day-time, except a short time in spring tides.

I am delighted with the improvements at Milford. It will surely be a great town, if we have peace, in three years; the houses rising up, like mushrooms, even in these difficult times. We allow any one to build—at their own expence—at an easy ground-rent, and to fall in at the expiration of three lives, or sixty years.

You may judge that, having two thousand acres all round the town, these inhabitants will want land for cows and horses, and gardens, &c. and, of course, I must be a gainer in the end.

I visited the two light-houses, and found them perfectly clean, and in good order: and I never could conceive the brilliant light that they give; one has sixteen reflected lights, and the other ten.

To-day, I go upon my last visit to Lord Milford; and, on Saturday, set out for Piccadilly: and where I am not without hopes of meeting your Lordship; as I think, in the manner you dispatch business, you will have completed all by Wednesday next, the day I shall probably be in London.

Charles Greville's kind compliments. The name of Nelson is in every mouth; and, indeed, we owe every thing to your judgment and exertions.

Adieu! God bless you. Ever your Lordship's affectionate friend, and obliged humble servant,

Wm. HAMILTON.

## XII.

Piccadilly, April 28th, 1802.

**MY DEAR LORD,**

Emma says—I must write a letter to you, of condolence for the heavy loss your Lordship has suffered.

When persons, in the prime of life, are carried off by accidents or sickness—or what is, I believe, oftener the case, by the ignorance and mistakes of the physicians—then, indeed, there is reason to lament! But as, in the case of your good Father, the lamp was suffered to burn out fairly, and that his sufferings were not great; and that, by his Son's glorious and unparalleled successes, he saw his family ennobled, and with the probability, in time, of its being amply rewarded, as it ought to have been long ago—his mind could not be troubled, in his latter moments, on account of the family he left behind him: and, as to his own peace of mind, at the moment of his dissolution, there can be no doubt, among those who ever had the honour of his acquaintance.

I have said more than I intended; but dare say, your Lordship had nearly the same thoughts—with the addition of the feelings of a dutiful Son, for the loss of a most excellent Father.

It is, however, now—as your Lordship is the Father of your Family—incumbent upon you to take particular care of your own health. Nay, you are, by the voice of the nation, its first prop and support.

Keep up your spirits; and, that you may long enjoy your well-earned honours, is the sincere wish of your Lordship's affectionate friend, and attached humble servant,

Wm. HAMILTON.

Letters

**FROM**

**LORD NELSON**

**TO**

## SIR WILLIAM HAMILTON, K.B.

Letters OF LORD NELSON, &c.

## I.

Bastia, May 24th, 1794.

**MY DEAR SIR,**

Will you have the goodness to forward the inclosed to Mr. Brand, and to present my letter to Lady Hamilton?

Every lover of his country will rejoice in our great and almost unexampled success, to the honour of my Lord Hood, and to the shame of those who opposed his endeavours to serve his country.

General Stewart, I am happy to say, is just arrived.

We shall now join, heart and hand, against Calvi. When conquered, I shall hope to pay my respects to your Excellency at Naples; which will give real pleasure to your very faithful, and obliged,

**HORATIO NELSON.**

## II.

Agamemnon, Leghorn,
March 11th, 1796.

**SIR,**

Mr. Wyndham having communicated to Mr. Udney the conversation of the French minister with the Tuscans, I cannot, being intrusted by the Admiral with the command of the small squadron in the Gulph of Genoa, but think it right for me to beg that your Excellency will apply for such vessels of war belonging to his Sicilian Majesty, as may be judged proper to cruize in the Gulph of Genoa, and particularly off the point of the Gulph of Especia. Xebecs, corvettes, and frigates, are the fittest to cruize; and the first have the great advantage of rowing, as well as sailing, I am told, very fast.

General [Acton] knows, full as well as myself, the vessels proper to prevent the disembarkation of troops on this coast; therefore, I shall not particularly point them out.

Last campaign, the word *flotilla* was misunderstood. I can only say, that all vessels which can sail and row must be useful; and, for small craft, Port Especia is a secure harbour.

Whatever is to be done, should be done speedily; for, by Mr. Wyndham's account, we have no time to lose.

If we have the proper vessels, I am confident, the French will not be able to bring their ten thousand men by sea; and; should they attempt to pass through the Genoese territories, I hope the Austrians will prevent them: but, however, should all our precautions not be able to prevent the enemy's possessing themselves of Leghorn, yet we are not to despair. Fourteen days from their entry, if the allied powers unite heartily, I am confident, we shall take them all prisoners. I am confident, it can—and, therefore, should such an unlucky event take place, as their possessing themselves of Leghorn, I hope, will—be done. I have sent to the Admiral.

I am, very lately, from off Toulon; where thirteen sail of the line, and five frigates, are ready for sea, and others fitting.

With my best respects to Lady Hamilton, believe me, dear Sir, your Excellency's most obedient servant,

**HORATIO NELSON.**

## III.

Vanguard, Syracuse, July 20th, 1798.

**MY DEAR SIR,**

It is an old saying, "The devil's children have the devil's luck." I cannot find—or, to this moment learn, beyond vague conjecture—where the French fleet are gone to. All my ill fortune, hitherto, has proceeded from want of frigates.

Off Cape Passaro, on the twenty-second of June, at day-light, I saw two frigates, which were supposed to be French; and it has been said, since, that a line-of-battle ship was to leeward of them, with the riches of Malta on board. But it was the destruction of the enemy, and not riches for myself, that I was seeking: these would have fell to me, if I had had frigates; but, except the ship of the line, I regard not all the riches in this world.

From my information off Malta, I believed they were gone to Egypt: therefore, on the twenty-eighth, I was communicating with Alexandria in Egypt; where I found the Turks preparing to resist them, but knew nothing beyond report.

From thence I stretched over to the coast of Caramania; where, not speaking a vessel who could give me information, I became distressed for the kingdom of the Two Sicilies: and, having gone a round of six hundred leagues, at this season of the year, (with a single ship, with an expedition incredible) here I am, as *ignorant* of the situation of the enemy as I was twenty-seven days ago!

I sincerely hope, the dispatches, which I understand are at Cape Passaro, will give me full information. I shall be able, for nine or ten weeks longer, to keep the fleet on active service, when we shall want provisions and stores. I send a paper on that subject, herewith.

Mr. Littledale is, I suppose, sent up by the Admiral to victual us, and I hope he will do it cheaper than any other person: but, if I find out that he charges more than the fair price, and has not the provisions of the very best quality, I will not take them; for, as no fleet has more fag than this, nothing but the best food, and greatest attention, can keep them healthy. At this moment, we have not one sick man in the fleet.

In about six days, I shall sail from hence: and, if I hear nothing more of the French, I shall go to the Archipelago; where, if they are gone towards Constantinople, I shall hear of them.

I shall go to Cyprus; and, if they are gone to Alexandretta, or any other part of Syria or Egypt, I shall get information.

You will, I am sure, and so will our country, easily conceive what has passed in my anxious mind; but I have this comfort, that I have no fault to accuse myself of: this bears me up, and this only.

I send you a paper, where a letter is fixed for different places: which I may leave at any place; and, except those who have the key, none can tell where I am gone to.

July 21.

The messenger is returned from Cape Passaro; and says, that your letters for me are returned to Naples. What a situation am I placed in! As yet, I can learn nothing of the enemy: therefore, I have no conjecture but that they are gone to Syria; and, at Cyprus, I hope to hear of them.

If they were gone to the westward, I rely that every place in Sicily would have information for me; for it is too important news to leave me in one moment's doubt about.

I have no frigate, or a sign of one. The masts, yards, &c. for the Vanguard, will I hope be prepared directly: for, should the French be so strongly secured in port that I cannot get at them, I shall immediately shift my flag into some other ship, and send the Vanguard to Naples to be refitted; for hardly any person but myself would have continued on service so long in such a wretched state.

I want to send a great number of papers to Lord St. Vincent; but I durst not trust any person here to carry them, even to Naples.

Pray, send a copy of my letter to Lord Spencer; he must be very anxious to hear of this fleet.

I have taken the liberty of troubling your Excellency with a letter for Lady Nelson. Pray, forward it for me; and believe me, with the greatest respect, your most obedient servant,

**HORATIO NELSON.**

Sent on shore, to the charge of the Governor of Syracuse.

## IV.

Vanguard, Syracuse, July 22d, 1798.

**MY DEAR SIR,**

I have had so much said about the King of Naples's orders only to admit three or four of the ships of our fleet into his ports, that I am astonished! I understood, that private orders, at least, would have been given for our free admission. If we are to be refused supplies, pray send me, by many vessels, an account, that I may in good time take the King's fleet to Gibraltar. Our treatment is scandalous, for a great nation to put up with; and the King's flag is insulted at every friendly port we look at.

I am, with the greatest respect, your most obedient servant,

**HORATIO NELSON.**

*P.S.* I do not complain of the want of attention in individuals, for all classes of people are remarkably attentive to us.

Sent on shore, to the charge of the Governor of Syracuse.

## V.

Vanguard, Mouth of the Nile,
August 8th, 1798.

**MY DEAR SIR,**

Almighty God has made me the happy instrument in destroying the enemy's fleet; which, I hope, will be a blessing to Europe.

You will have the goodness to communicate this happy event to all the courts in Italy; for my head is so indifferent, that I can scarcely scrawl this letter.

Captain Capel, who is charged with my dispatches for England, will give you every information. Pray, put him in the quickest mode of getting home.

You will not send, by post, any particulars of this action, as I should be sorry to have any accounts get home before my dispatches.

I hope there will be no difficulty in our getting refitted at Naples. Culloden must be instantly hove down, and Vanguard all new masts and bowsprit. Not more than four or five sail of the line will probably come to Naples; the rest will go with the prizes to Gibraltar.

As this army never will return, I hope to hear the Emperor has regained the whole of Italy.

With every good wish, believe me, dear Sir, your most obliged and affectionate

**HORATIO NELSON.**

9th August.

I have intercepted all Buonaparte's dispatches going to France. This army is in a scrape, and will not get out of it.

## VI.

August 12th, 1798.

**MY DEAR SIR,**

As the greater part of this squadron is going down the Mediterranean, we shall not want the quantity of wine or bread ordered; therefore, what is not already prepared had better be put a stop to. I will settle all the matter, if ever I live to see Naples.

I have the satisfaction to tell you, the French army have got a complaint amongst them—caused by the heat, and nothing but water—which will make Egypt the grave of the greatest part.

Ever your's, faithfully,

**HORATIO NELSON.**

# VII.

Vanguard, off Malta;
October 24th, 1798.

**MY DEAR SIR,**

I am just arrived off this place; where I found Captain Ball, and the Marquis de Niza. From those officers, I do not find such an immediate prospect of getting possession of the town as the ministers at Naples seem to think. All the country, it is true, is in possession of the islanders; and, I believe, the French have not many luxuries in the town; but, as yet, their bullocks are not eat up.

The Marquis tells me, the islanders want arms, victuals, mortars, and cannon, to annoy the town. When I get the elect of the people on board, I shall desire them to draw up a memorial for the King of Naples, stating their wants and desires, which I shall bring with me.

The Marquis sails for Naples to-morrow morning. Till he is gone, I shall not do any thing about the island; but I will be fully master of that subject before I leave this place.

God bless you! is the sincere prayer of

**HORATIO NELSON.**

# VIII.

Vanguard, off Malta,
October 27th, 1798.

**MY DEAR SIR WILLIAM,**

Although I believe I shall be at Naples before the cutter, yet I should be sorry to omit acknowledging your kind letter of the twenty-sixth.

When I come to Naples, I can have nothing pleasant to say of the conduct of his Sicilian Majesty's ministers towards the inhabitants of Malta, who wish to be under the dominion of their legitimate Sovereign. The total neglect and indifference with which they have been treated, appears to me *cruel* in the extreme.

Had not the English supplied fifteen hundred stand of arms, with bayonets, cartouch-boxes, and ammunition, &c. &c. and the Marquis supplied some few, and kept the spirit of those brave islanders from falling off, they must long ago have bowed again to the French yoke.

Could you, my dear Sir William, have believed, after what General Acton and the Marquis de Gallo had said, in our various conversations relative to this island, that nothing had been sent by the Governor of Syracuse—*secretly* (was the word to us) or openly—to this island? And, I am farther assured, that the Governor of Syracuse never had any orders sent him to supply the smallest article.

I beg your Excellency will state this, in confidence, to General Acton. I shall, most assuredly, tell it to the King! The justice I owe myself, now I feel employed in the service of their Sicilian Majesties, demands it of me; and, also, the duty I owe our gracious King, in order to shew that I am doing my utmost to comply with his royal commands.

As I have before stated, had it not been for the English, long, long ago, the Maltese must have been overpowered. Including the fifteen hundred stand of arms given by us, not more than three thousand are in the island. I wonder how they have kept on the defensive so long.

The Emerald will sail—in twenty-four hours after my arrival—for Malta; at least, two thousand stand of small arms complete, ammunition, &c. &c. should be sent by her. This is wanted, to defend themselves: for offence, two or three large mortars; fifteen hundred shells, with all necessaries; and, perhaps, a few artillery—two ten-inch howitzers, with a thousand shells. The Bormola, and all the left side of the harbour, with this assistance, will fall. Ten thousand men are required to defend those works, the French can only spare twelve hundred; therefore, a vigorous assault in many parts, some one must succeed.

But, who have the government of Naples sent to lead or encourage these people? A very good—and, I dare say, brave—old man; enervated, and shaking with the palsy. This is the sort of man that they have sent; without any supply, without even a promise of protection, and without his bringing any answer to the repeated respectful memorials of these people to their Sovereign.

I know, their Majesties must feel hurt, when they hear these truths. I may be thought presuming; but, I trust, General Acton will forgive an honest seaman for telling plain truths. *As for the other minister, I do not understand him;* we are different men! He has been bred in a court, and I in a rough element. But, I believe, my heart is as susceptible of the finer feelings as his, and as compassionate for the distress of those who look up to me for protection.

The officer sent here should have brought supplies, promises of protection, and an answer from the King to their memorials: he should have been a man of judgment, bravery, and *activity*. He should be the first to lead them to glory; and the last, when necessary, to retreat: the first to mount the walls of the Bormola, and never to quit it. This is the man to send. Such, many such, are to be found. If he succeeds, promise him rewards; my life for it, the business would soon be over.

God bless you! I am anxious to get this matter finished. I have sent Ball, this day, to summon Goza; if it resists, I shall send on shore, and batter down the castle.

Three vessels, loaded with bullocks, &c. for the garrison, were taken yesterday; from Tripoli ten more are coming, but we shall have them.

I had almost forgot to mention, that orders should be immediately given, that no quarantine should be laid on boats going to the coast of Sicily for corn. At present, as a matter of favour, they have *fourteen* days only. Yesterday, there was only four days bread in the island. Luckily, we got hold of a vessel loaded with wheat, and sent her into St. Paul's.

Once more, God bless you! and ever believe me, your obliged and affectionate

## HORATIO NELSON.

This day, I have landed twenty barrels of gunpowder (two thousand eight hundred pounds) at Malta.

## IX.

Palermo, January 10th, 1800.

### SIR,

Your Excellency having had the goodness to communicate to me a dispatch from General Acton; together with several letters from *Girganti*, giving an account that a violence had been committed, in that port, by the seizing, and carrying off to Malta, two vessels loaded with corn—I beg leave to express to your Excellency my real concern, that even the appearance of the slightest disrespect should be offered, by any officers under my command, to the flag of his Sicilian Majesty: and I must request your Excellency to state fully to General Acton, that the act ought not to be considered as any intended disrespect to his Sicilian Majesty; but as an act of the most absolute and imperious necessity, either that the island of Malta should have been delivered up to the French, or that the King's orders should be anticipated for these vessels carrying their cargoes of corn to Malta.

I trust, that the government of this country will never again force any of our Royal Master's servants to so unpleasant an alternative.

I have the honour to be, with the greatest respect, your Excellency's most obedient and faithful servant,

**B.N.**

# X.

March 8th, 1800.

**MY DEAR SIR WILLIAM,**

I thank you kindly for all your letters and good wishes. It is my determination, *my health requiring it*, to come to Palermo, and to stay two weeks with you.

I must again urge, that four gunb-oats may be ordered for the service of Malta; they will most essentially assist in the reduction of the place, by preventing small vessels from getting in or out.

I think, from the enemy, on the night of the fourth, trying and getting out for a short distance, a very fast-sailing polacca, that Vaubois is extremely anxious to send dispatches to France, to say he cannot much longer hold out: and, if our troops, as Captain Blackwood thinks, are coming from Gibraltar and Minorca, I have no idea the enemy will hold out a week.

I beg General Acton will order the gun-boats.

Troubridge has got the jaundice, and is very ill.

As I shall so very soon see you, I shall only say, that I am ever, your obliged and affectionate

**BRONTE NELSON.**

# XI.

Palermo, March 30th, 1800.

**MY DEAR SIR WILLIAM,**

As, from the orders I have given, to all the ships under my command, to arrest and bring into port all the vessels and troops returning by convention with the Porte to France—and as the Russian ships have similar orders—I must request that your Excellency will endeavour to arrange with the government of this country, how in the first instance they are to be treated and received in the ports of the Two Sicilies: for, it is obvious, I can do nothing more than bring them into port; and, if they are kept on board ship, the fever will make such ravages as to be little short of the plague.

It is a very serious consideration for this country, either to receive them, or let them pass; when they would invade, probably, these kingdoms. In my present situation in the King's fleet, I have only to obey; had I been, as before, in the command, I should have gone one short and direct road to avert this great evil: *viz.* to have sent a letter to the French, and the Grand Vizir, in Egypt, that I would not, on any consideration, permit a single Frenchman to leave Egypt—and I would do it at the risk of even creating a coldness, for the moment, with the Turks.

Of two evils, choose the least; and nothing can be so horrid, as permitting that horde of thieves to return to Europe.

If all the wise heads had left them to God Almighty, after the bridge was broke, all would have ended well! For I differ entirely with my Commander in Chief, in wishing they were permitted to return to France; and, likewise, with Lord Elgin, in the great importance of removing them from Egypt. No; there they should perish! has ever been the firm determination of your Excellency's most obedient and faithful servant,

**BRONTE NELSON OF THE NILE.**

## XII.

Palermo, April 10th, 1800.

**MY DEAR SIR WILLIAM,**

Reports are brought to me, that the Spanish ships of war in this port are preparing to put to sea; a circumstance which must be productive of very unpleasant consequences, to both England and this country.

It is fully known, with what exactness I have adhered to the neutrality of this port; for, upon our arrival here, from Naples, in December 1798, from the conduct of his Catholic Majesty's minister, I should have been fully justified in seizing those ships.

We know, that one object of the Spanish fleet, combined with the French, was to wrest entirely from the hands of his Sicilian Majesty his kingdoms of the Two Sicilies.

The Spaniards are, by bad councils, the tools of the French; and, of course, the bitter enemy of his Sicilian Majesty and family.

The conduct I have pursued towards these ships, circumstanced as they are, has been moderate, and truly considerate towards his Sicilian Majesty.

The time is now come—that, profiting of my forbearance, the Spanish ships are fitting for sea. It is not possible, if they persist in their preparations, that I can avoid attacking them, even in the port of Palermo; for they never can, or shall, be suffered to go to sea, and placed in a situation of assisting the French, against not only Great Britain, but also the Two Sicilies.

I have, therefore, to request, that your Excellency will convey my sentiments on this very delicate subject to his Sicilian Majesty's ministers, that they may take measures to prevent such a truly unpleasant event happening; which would be as much against my wish as it can be against their's: and I request that your Excellency will, through its proper channel, assure his Sicilian Majesty, that his safety and honour is as dear to me as that of our Royal Master.

I have the honour to be, with the greatest respect, my dear Sir William, your Excellency's most affectionate, humble servant,

**BRONTE NELSON OF THE NILE.**

CPSIA information can be obtained
at www.ICGtesting.com
Printed in the USA
LVHW030003281222
735835LV00002B/587